ENDNOTES

AN INTIMATE LOOK
AT THE END OF LIFE

RUTH E. RAY

Columbia University Press   *New York*

Columbia University Press

Publishers Since 1893

New York   Chichester, West Sussex

Copyright ©2008 Columbia University Press

All rights reserved

Library of Congress Cataloging-in-Publication Data

Ray, Ruth E., 1954–

   Endnotes: an intimate look at the end of life / Ruth E. Ray.

      p. cm. — (End-of-life care : a series)

   ISBN 978-0-231-14460-5 (cloth : alk. paper) — ISBN 978-0-231-14461-2
(pbk. : alk. paper) — 978-0-231-51785-0 (ebook)

   1. Love in old age.   2. Older people—Psychology.   3. Man-woman
relationships.   4. Gerontologists.   5. Death.   I. Title.   II. Series.

   HQ1061.R32   2008

   306.7084′6—dc22

                                                      2007046527

ENDNOTES

END-OF-LIFE CARE

END-OF-LIFE CARE: A SERIES
Series editor: Virginia E. Richardson

We all confront end-of-life issues. As people live longer and suffer from more chronic illnesses, all of us face difficult decisions about death, dying, and terminal care. This series aspires to articulate the issues surrounding end-of-life care in the twenty-first century. It will be a resource for practitioners and scholars who seek information about advance directives, hospice, palliative care, bereavement, and other death-related topics. The interdisciplinary approach makes the series invaluable for social workers, physicians, nurses, attorneys, and pastoral counselors.

The press seeks manuscripts that reflect the interdisciplinary, biopsychosocial essence of end-of-life care. We welcome manuscripts that address specific topics on ethical dilemmas in end-of-life care, death, and dying among marginalized groups, palliative care, spirituality, and end-of-life care in special medical areas, such as oncology, AIDS, diabetes, and transplantation. While writers should integrate theory and practice, the series is open to diverse methodologies and perspectives.

Joan Berzoff and Phyllis R. Silverman, *Living with Dying: A Handbook for End-of-Life Healthcare Practitioners*

Virginia E. Richardson and Amanda S. Barusch, *Gerontological Practice for the Twenty-first Century: A Social Work Perspective*

To live from the mind is to balance in uncertainty on a high wire. . . .
We may have to surrender, as do artists of all kinds, to a looser life and
a more liberated imagination.

—Thomas Moore,
Original Self: Living with Paradox and Originality

CONTENTS

Contents

PREFACE

Endnotes, for academic researchers, are the supplemental references and comments that appear at the end of a scholarly paper. In this book, I describe events that occurred at the end of a research project that took place during the summer and fall of 1996. *Endnotes* is about my relationship with one man who participated in the study and who later became my close friend. To be frank, I fell in love with this man, and he fell in love with me. As it turns out, then, *Endnotes* is a love story, told from the perspective of a midlife woman, a feminist, and a gerontologist working to "befriend" old age. I offer it as homage to my friend Paul and to all people who live in nursing homes.

I call *Endnotes* a memoir because I have drawn on personal recollections, along with some of Paul's life stories, to construct the story of our relationship. Literary critic Nancy K. Miller defines "memoirs" as "documents about building an identity—how we come to be who we are as individuals," which, for women writers especially, often involves the author's writing herself in and out of others' stories. Miller's understanding of memoir as "a dialogue enacted with other selves" is what I have tried to create here.[1] By retelling Paul's stories and re-creating shared experiences in the form of conversations, I illustrate who Paul was at the end of his life, as well as who I was in relationship to Paul.

Memoirs take many shapes and have fluid boundaries, often combining autobiography and biography. Since memoir "encompasses both acts of memory and acts of recording—personal reminiscences and documentation," it is both fictional and nonfictional, which is to say that while everything in this book is true, I have certainly not remembered or recorded all that happened, and I have combined and rearranged events to suit my purposes.[2] I have also changed the names of people and places and slightly altered some descriptions to preserve anonymity. *Endnotes* is therefore a combination of fact and imaginative recall, enhanced by research in gerontology and related fields. It is what Linda Flower, my colleague in rhetoric and composition studies, calls a "hybrid text."[3] Hopefully, I have taken the best aspects of several different kinds of texts—autobiography, biography, reminiscence and life review, personal essay, ethnographic research report—to create a text that is informative and enlightening to a variety of readers, including those who previously have shown little interest in aging or old age.

In 1996, I was just beginning my career in gerontology. While trying to understand the experiences of aging through my research and through interactions with old people, I was also exploring my new identity as an age researcher. I was forty-two years old and in the midst of an academic career move from English professor to gerontologist. I had no idea where this intellectual journey would lead or what kind of gerontologist I would become. Gerontology as a discipline was (and still is) driven by the medical professions and the social sciences. As an English professor trained in rhetoric and linguistics, I had to determine for myself what role I might play in generating knowledge about old age. My feminist ethic required that I engage in some form of praxis—an integration of research, theory, and practice—that would generate positive consequences for the people and places I studied. In Harry R. Moody's words, then, *Endnotes* explores "the *subjectivity* of the life world" in a nursing home—merging research, theory, and personal experience with the intention of changing readers' minds about the potential in old age.[4]

In terms of the academic literature, this book fits within the categories of feminist gerontology and narrative gerontology. Feminist gerontologists conduct research and write theory to increase our understanding of gender differences and diversity in aging, old age, and age relations.[5] Narrative gerontologists do a lot of face-to-face work, interviewing old people, facilitating reminiscence groups, and recording conversations. In an effort to understand age from the perspective of old people themselves, they often collect and analyze life stories. What motivated Malcolm Cowley to write his memoir, *The View from 80*, is what motivates most narrative gerontologists: "Those self-appointed experts on old age [know] the literature but not the life."[6] My first book in gerontology, *Beyond Nostalgia: Aging and Life Story Writing*, based on observations of and interviews with senior citizen writing groups, is a work of narrative gerontology in which I explore the subjective meanings of age through the writings of older people. I would say that *Endnotes* is a parallel text to—or a subtext of—*Beyond Nostalgia*. While *Beyond Nostalgia* is a scholarly text in which I describe a somewhat distant relationship to older people and their lives, *Endnotes* is a personal text in which I describe my subjective responses to one old person in particular. Taken together, the two books reflect an understanding I have come to over the past few years: gerontologists, at least some of us, have an ethical responsibility to function as social-change agents, broadening and deepening public perceptions and providing alternative images and conceptions of aging and old age. I refer to this cause as "narrative for social change," and I have explained elsewhere that it involves telling countercultural stories about aging and old age, celebrating the unexpected and the inexplicable in these stories, engaging as researchers and writers in the critical self-reflection and self-reflexivity needed to work through our own age anxieties, and, in the process, changing not only how we and others *think* about aging but also how we *feel* about it.[7] This ambitious enterprise is my goal in writing *Endnotes*.

In 1996, however, I did not realize that deep emotional involvement would become central to my training as a gerontologist. At that time, I was facilitating writing groups in several senior centers and nursing homes, interviewing writers, recording how they interacted in these groups, and analyzing the form and content of their stories and storytelling. That summer, I had the opportunity to develop a writing group at the Bedford Nursing Home. The director of nursing asked a nurse researcher at the Wayne State University Institute of Gerontology to design an intervention to help residents in the nursing home deal with what the literature in nursing called "relocation stress," a response to moving from one home to another. The old Bedford was to be abandoned for a new facility built on the same grounds, and residents were experiencing mixed emotions— excitement, anxiety, anticipation, insecurity. I was a scholar-in-residence at the institute during my fellowship period, and the nurse researcher asked if I would develop writing groups to serve as the intervention. She and her graduate students proposed to conduct a scientific study around the groups, evaluating whether our sessions had any impact on residents' mental or physical health. I was curious whether the researchers would find any scientific evidence to support the value of my writing groups, so I agreed to participate.

For my part in the project, I developed a series of four one-hour sessions, to be held from mid-July to mid-August, around the themes of "home" and "transitions." Two groups, each with ten to twelve participants, would meet on Wednesdays, one in the morning and one in the afternoon. I began each session the same way, by reading a poem or passage aloud. I then asked group members to write something inspired by the passage. The volunteers and I moved around the group, assisting members in composing short responses. I ended each session by reading aloud what everyone had written. Back at my office, I would type up the writings and return the following week, circulating the typed versions for editorial changes. At the end of the four weeks, I put all the edited writings together in a spiral-bound book called "Reflections on Home" and distributed copies to the group members, the nursing home administration, and staff members. On the cover of the book, I juxtaposed two pictures: a line drawing of the old nursing home and an architect's rendering of the new one.

What were the outcomes of this "experiment"? The research team measured residents' depression levels, number of falls, use of pain medications, and changes in attitude and behavior. In the end, they found no statistically significant differences between residents who participated in the writing groups and those in control groups who had not participated. These results were never published, and the researchers moved on to other projects. I, however, continued to talk with people in the nursing home, not as a researcher but a friendly visitor. For me, it was life after the study, rather than the study itself, that bore fruit. This book offers some of what I learned.

ENDNOTES

I PASSIONATE SCHOLARSHIP

For many academic readers, my blurring of personal and professional boundaries in writing this book will be controversial. Indeed, an early reviewer of the manuscript commented, "It is exactly the kind of work that one would not expect to be written by a professional gerontologist." I take this as a compliment. In this opening chapter, I offer a rationale for the intimate memoir you are about to read, and I suggest that the field of gerontology, as well as the world of readers outside of academe, would benefit from even more of what I am calling "passionate scholarship." By this I mean research and writing on significant topics that resonate personally with the author. Passionate scholarship is heartfelt and emotional but also intellectually rigorous and well documented. Passionate scholarship, which I have gleaned from feminist scholars and social critics, including Martha Holstein and Meredith Minkler in gerontology, Toril Moi in literary criticism, and Laurel Richardson in sociology, is

explicit as to the author's value commitments,
expressive of a particular standpoint (intellectual, political, and/or moral),

methodologically flexible (even playful),
demonstrative of personal and experiential knowing, in conjunction with
    intellectual knowing,
reflective and reflexive,
challenging to the status quo,
social-change oriented,
emotionally engaged, rather than emotionally indifferent,
presented in a way that reflects the distinct voice of the writer/scholar,
    while still acknowledging the voices and viewpoints of others.

Above all, as Holstein and Minkler explain, passionate scholarship "does not aim for control or domination, nor even for certainty, but for the freedom to pursue questions, to challenge assumptions, to hear and respect a multitude of voices, and to take engaged critique as a long-term commitment."[1]

Elsewhere I have described passionate scholarship in the narrative mode, pointing out the need for more "narrating gerontologists" who engage in critical self-reflection while telling stories about themselves *of a certain age* interacting with others of different ages as they tell their stories. Through these narrative relationships, the gerontologist tries to make sense of the experience of aging, generating "empathy and compassion, as well as intellectual understanding, and [evoking] a change of consciousness on the part of the researcher *and* the reader."[2] The ideal outcome of such work is increased social justice—respect and equitable treatment for people of all ages and abilities.

There is no better time than the first half of the twenty-first century for gerontologists to engage in passionate scholarship. The most recent U.S. census data assert that in 2000 there were more than 30 million Americans age sixty-five to eighty-four and 4 million Americans age eighty-five and older. By 2030, the number of Americans in both age groups will have more than doubled. By 2050, the growth in the sixty-five to eighty-four age group will have leveled off, but the number of Americans age eighty-five will have doubled again. In short, those we now call the "oldest old" will become the fastest growing segment of the population. As the feminist activist Cynthia Rich reminds us, however, an increase in numbers doesn't necessarily lead to social change. "Will it matter that the baby boomers are aging?" she asks. "Well, there may be more of us old women every day, but if numbers translated into power, women and people of color would rule the world. I don't put faith in numbers."[3] Clearly, this time and place in history are calling gerontologists to action. The complex issues presented by an aging society will require a higher level of thinking, feeling, and knowing than we have demonstrated so far. How will we prepare for these challenges? Some of the most advanced thinkers in the field have called for a renewal of the "gerontological imagination."

The Gerontological Imagination

Many gerontologists are already aware of our increased social responsibilities and the need for new ways of responding. In 2006, the theme of the 59th annual conference of the Gerontological Society of America (GSA) was "Education and the Gerontological Imagination." In their opening address, GSA president Charles Longino and GSA executive director Carol Schutz evoked the title of sociologist C. Wright Mills's famous 1959 book, *The Sociological Imagination*, in which Mills argued that because personal lives reflect public issues, social research should proceed on the micro (individual) and macro (social) levels simultaneously. Mills's larger purpose in writing the book was to encourage social researchers to think bigger—to imagine themselves as public intellectuals who could effect social change. To achieve this larger purpose, academics would have to break out of their traditional modes of thinking (Mills targeted theoreticism and empiricism) and encompass multiple ways of knowing and responding, including creative and imaginative approaches more often associated with the humanities. In 2006, following Mills,

Longino and Schutz called for more "imaginative responses" to the individual and social issues generated by an aging society. They took this to mean, among other things, a merging of humanistic and scientific approaches to the study of old age.

Nearly fifteen years earlier, in an article in the *International Journal of Aging and Human Development*, the gerontologists Carroll Estes, Elizabeth Binney, and Richard Culbertson laid the groundwork for developing more imaginative responses to aging societies. They, too, drew their inspiration from Mills in identifying the characteristics of a "gerontological imagination" that would bring social awareness to the study of aging. Following a historical review of the main theoretical paradigms operating in gerontology since 1945, Estes, Binney, and Culbertson offered three likely scenarios for older Americans in the next fifty years:

1. Costly medical measures will prolong life for many who would otherwise have died.
2. Chronic diseases, once fatal, will be successfully treated, resulting in fewer deaths but leaving people to live with chronic illness for a longer time.
3. Lifestyle changes will diminish the chance of acquiring some diseases and will decrease comorbidity (independent but coexisting conditions, such as heart disease and diabetes); however, people will continue to develop nonfatal conditions that are life altering but not life threatening.

Taken together, these scenarios suggest that more people will live longer with disabilities. Meanwhile, segments of the population will continue to experience unequal access to health care and an escalating "intergenerational war" in which the old are pitted against the young in a fight for limited resources. Additionally, changes in the workforce, later childbearing, an inflated cost of living, and multigenerational care responsibilities will create more hardship for a larger portion of the population. All of this will occur simultaneously as the government cuts public assistance through Social Security and Medicare.[4]

Gerontologists would best respond to these problems, following Mills, with vigorous social analyses that culminate in recommendations for individual and systemic change in the ways we respond to health care, social welfare, and the experience of aging. The work of gerontologists would circulate in the general public, as well as in the academy, and would be accessible to a wide readership of experts and laypeople. But Estes, Binney, and Culbertson claim that gerontology as a field is not prepared to respond in this way. It has, instead, been caught up in the politics of academic legitimization, becoming ever more scientific ("hard") and less social and humanistic ("soft") and renouncing its social responsibilities for financial rewards and prestige in the academy. As a result, the authors fear that gerontology is "in danger of 'selling its soul.'" They offer the "gerontological imagination" as both critique and intervention. Drawing on Mills, the authors argue that "personal experiences and troubles related to health and the aging process need to be linked with larger social questions of how the political and economic systems are interconnected with these troubles." This kind of scholarship requires that gerontologists "move away from the biomedicalization, individualism, particularism, and reductionism that have infected gerontology" and recognize that our research must have "real effects on real people."[5]

Imaginative Research and Writing

I take these calls for a gerontological imagination seriously, and I agree with them. But how might interpretive social scientists and humanists like me respond? How can we use our skills to increase the social relevance of gerontology? In search of an answer to this question, I turned to the appendix of Mills's book, along with the writings of contemporary feminist scholars who are known for their passionate scholarship. I have concluded that scholars who are trained to read closely, to observe and interpret at the microlevel, can serve as a "soulful" reminder of the potential in research to both reflect and affect the human concerns of "real people." Such scholars often study the workings of the imagination. We can therefore help our colleagues in gerontology understand, value, and exercise their own imaginations.

One of my unique contributions, as a writer and longtime teacher of writing, is to remind gerontologists that writing is a natural pathway to the imagination. Indeed, in the appendix of his book, Mills explains how he used writing to develop his own imagination in becoming what he calls an "intellectual craftsman." The intellectual craftsman uses all of his or her intellectual, experiential, and emotional resources to probe, understand, explain, articulate, and respond to the social issues of the day, merging theory and research with speculation, intellectual play, and emotional response. Mills describes two approaches by which intellectual craftsmen develop the sociological imagination: first, through close observation and reflection, they develop a deep understanding of themselves as *human beings* working in their field, and second, they pay close attention to how they and others use language. What Mills observed in the late 1950s is just as true today: "The most admirable thinkers within the scholarly community do not split their work from their lives. They seem to take both too seriously to allow such dissociation, and they want to use each for the enrichment of the other." For Mills, reflective writing was the best way for an intellectual craftsman to integrate life and work. He suggested that new scholars, especially, keep a "file"—which he acknowledged was another name for "journal"—in which they document what they are doing in their research, alongside what they are experiencing as a person. This file ultimately becomes the source of all deeply held opinions and the taproot for passionate scholarship. By juxtaposing personal experience with scholarly reflection, the writer observes the germination of new ideas and develops trust and confidence in the workings of her own mind which, as Mills says, is "indispensable to originality in any intellectual pursuit."[6] Mills also explains in detail how an intellectual craftsman takes notes on others' work and uses these to generate her ideas and connections. He describes the intimate connection between language and thought and urges scholars to use language carefully and conscientiously to search for just the right words and phrases; to define and redefine key terms and then use them consistently; to articulate the logical connections between their own and others' ideas; and to consider the full implications of their arguments. This attention to language not only makes the scholar a better thinker, but also a more persuasive, impassioned writer.

One reason for the longevity of Mills's book is that he practices what he preaches. Not only are his arguments brilliant, but they are also beautifully executed, with a sense of urgency and purpose. Besides that, he is wickedly funny and irreverent, while maintaining intellectual rigor. Mills advocates for a prose style that is accessible to academic and nonacademic readers alike, and he achieves this goal easily by assuming the persona of a writer who is comfortable with what he knows and who *wants* to communicate it to others. Mills argues against the "turgid" style of the typical academic treatise, claiming that the complexity of such texts is not so much a reflection of the subject matter as the writers' "confusion" about their intellectual status. Mills's pithy advice is perhaps even more relevant for today's scholars: "To overcome the academic *prose* you have first to overcome the academic *pose*."[7] This "pose" can be conquered by thinking of one's audience as a variety of intelligent people who have a *right* to know what you know. Mills advises the intellectual craftsman to speak to this audience from the center of his or her own experience and reasoning, saying, in effect, "I have found out something. I want to tell you about it and how I found it out." As simple and obvious as this sounds, it is an unaccustomed stance for most academic writers. The voice behind the usual academic text, especially if theory driven, is more like this: "I have been thinking about some very complex ideas. Most people won't understand them, so I won't even bother explaining. I'm pretty much writing for myself and a handful of other people whom I want to impress with my intelligence."

In recent years, many feminist scholars, myself included, have been working to overcome this pose, which strikes us as arrogant and self-serving. We try to make our writing intelligible to a broader audience, and we offer both personal and political reasons for doing so. "Power" and "voice" are significant concerns for us, as we often write about marginalized and oppressed individuals and groups. The feminist sociologist Laurel Richardson reminds us that whenever we write *about* something or someone or *for* something, we are exercising our authority and our privilege; such writing is therefore a "site of moral responsibility." As she sees it, feminist writers have an ethical obligation to ask themselves, "How can we use our skills and privileges to advance the cause of the nonprivileged?" In relation to overcoming the academic pose, especially when writing theory, Richardson invites us to think about the relationship between writer and reader in terms of power: "How one writes one's theory is not simply a theoretical matter. The theoretical inscribes a social order, power relationships, and the subjective state of the theorist." In response to the challenge of empowering readers, as well as the subjects of her research, Richardson experiments with form and content in her sociological writing, combining personal experience with abstract reasoning and using creative, open-ended, polyvocal forms of expression, including imaginary dialogues, poems, and plays. Richardson offers her reader-friendly research and theory as a critique of and substitute for the "numbing, disaffective, disembodied, schizoid sensibilities characteristic of phallocentristic social science."[8] Her description of feminist postmodernist writing closely parallels Mills's description of the intellectual craftsman's writing, and it is the kind of writing I have tried to develop in *Endnotes*.

For Richardson and other feminist academics, the choice of an accessible speaking voice and the deliberate use of "ordinary language" to write scholarly texts is an enactment of feminist praxis—theory into practice. In the chapter titled "The Personal and the Philosophical" in her book *What Is a Woman?* the feminist critic Toril Moi advises feminist scholars not to "get lost in meaningless questions and pointless arguments" but instead to "raise genuine questions about things that really matter." She explores what it means to read and write as a feminist by examining the works of the French existentialist Simone de Beauvoir, using the language theories of Ludwig Wittgenstein and J.L. Austin. Moi argues against the common assumption that academic writing and ordinary language and experience are somehow at odds. Along with the existentialists, she believes that our acts, including our uses of language, define us. That is, we are not what we *say* but what we *do* in our actions and our language practices. Moi also argues for the analysis of concrete cases as a method for understanding complex social realities, along with the use of personal experience, told in a personal voice, to "solve problems" of social significance. Personal stories should be illuminating and should invite us to think about substantive matters. They should evoke "the power of thought developed through careful examination of a particular case."[9] This is autobiography used in the service of social analysis, rather than autobiography used for personal exploration alone. It is what I have attempted to do in writing *Endnotes* as an auto/biography informed by critical research on old age and nursing home reform.

In terms of establishing a voice as a feminist scholar, Moi raises thoughtful questions that should concern all scholars who wish to write passionately for social change: "Is it possible to write theory in a way that overcomes the apparent conflict between the general and the particular, the third person and the first person? How do I write theory in a personal voice? How do I write theory without losing myself and alienating my readers in the process?" Trained as a literary critic, Moi addresses these questions through a close analysis of Beauvoir's *The Second Sex*, considered in the context of Beauvoir's work habits. Moi points out that Beauvoir, writing in the male-dominated fields of philosophy and literary criticism during the

1930s and 1940s, developed a working style that helped her integrate her personal and academic lives. Beauvoir wrote primarily in cafes, where she also "met her friends and lovers and conducted her professional life. The way she organized her everyday life reinforced her sense that life and philosophy were interconnected."[10] Such interconnection takes courage and creativity, but it is the key to writing passionate scholarship and developing the gerontological imagination.

Ethical Concerns

Endnotes is written to illustrate the interconnections between feminist studies, gerontological research, and my personal life as a middle-aged woman in a relationship with an old man. This approach raises a number of ethical and professional issues. As Gesa Kirsch notes in her introduction to *Ethical Dilemmas in Feminist Research*, inevitably, those of us who follow feminist principles will encounter ethical dilemmas in our research and writing. We will come up against those who disagree with our values (social justice for underrepresented groups); our goals (social critique and social change); and our methods (reflexivity, attention to the affective domain, and a focus on lived experience, especially in domestic settings, with the purpose of validating the significance of ordinary life.)[11] Because feminists are concerned with power—all forms of domination and subordination—we sometimes write about socially disempowered individuals and groups in ways that elevate them. I have tried to demonstrate all these values in writing *Endnotes*, recognizing that some readers will take issue with this approach.

The federal government imposes ethical guidelines on academic researchers who work with "vulnerable subjects"—people in various states of dependency. Academic research proposals undergo intense scrutiny by the internal review boards of universities, whose job is to ensure that the four principles of biomedical ethics are followed: respect for others' autonomy (the right to choose freely); nonmaleficence (the promise to do no harm to others); beneficence (the promise to protect and defend the rights of others and to prevent harm whenever possible); and justice (the promise to treat everyone equally and fairly).[12]

There is no comparable standard of ethics for those of us who write memoirs and auto/biographies, but literary critic G. Thomas Couser argues that the standards of biomedical ethics should guide our decisions. He finds that auto/biographical writing and cases of medical ethics frequently address the same issues and are comparable in many ways. For example, auto/biographies are often "quality of life" writings based on close observation of a vulnerable other in order to distinguish that person's sense of worth and value in the face of disability, age, or both. Couser introduces the term "auto/bio/ethics," which encapsulates the "vital relations" between "auto/biography—which refers to intimate life writing that focuses on the relation between the writer and a significant other—with bioethics".[13] The questions he raises in his preface to *Vulnerable Subjects: Ethics and Life Writing* get directly to the core of my own concerns about writing *Endnotes* as a memoir that involves vulnerable others:

> Where does the right to express and represent oneself begin to infringe on another's right to privacy? How shall the desires of the self be weighed against the demands of the other, concerns for aesthetics with concerns for ethics? Is it necessary, or at least desirable, to obtain consent or permission from those to be represented? When consent cannot be obtained, what constraints, if any, should apply to intimate life writing? . . . Are auto/biographers obliged to "do good"—or at least do no harm—to those they represent? Can harm to minor characters in one's autobiography be dismissed as unavoidable and trivial? If life writing necessarily involves violating the privacy of others and possibly harming them, what values might offset such ethical liabilities? . . . What constitutes appropriation or even expropriation of someone else's story?[14]

These questions raise important issues related to privacy, consent, and the relative "benefits" of personal writing that represents others. Taken together, Couser's questions raise the primary ethical concern of all life writers: To what degree, and with what consequences, is our writing an act of betrayal? This is a question that concerns me, and it deserves exploration here, at the beginning of my own memoir involving vulnerable subjects.

In terms of their right to privacy, ideally I would have gotten consent from all major and minor characters (or their guardians), including Paul and his son, other residents of the nursing home, their family members, and staff members who are represented in the narrative. Adhering to this standard would have required my knowing in 1996 that I was going to publish a memoir and that certain characters were likely to appear in it, which was not the case. Retrospective consent was a possibility, but I chose not to seek it as the years passed, believing that I had made all characters (with the possible exception of Paul) sufficiently anonymous so as to do no harm. I understand that the impairments of nursing home residents do subject them to harm (in the form of exploitation) and render them vulnerable to misrepresentation. I respond to this concern in the same way that Couser addresses the ethics of John Bayley writing about his philosopher wife's dementia in *Elegy for Iris*: If the representation is respectful and, rather than harming the subject's reputation, actually "ascribes value to what seems an inherently undignified condition," then it carries an integrity of purpose that makes it "ethical."[15] Although Iris was still living when John published his book, most of the people represented in *Endnotes* are now deceased. This fact is relevant because, legally, autonomy and the right to privacy no longer apply after death. Of course, the social and emotional concerns of living family members remain, and I can only hope that if a family member should read this account and recognize a deceased relative (or even him- or herself), the reader will feel that a greater good (such as more enlightened responses to dementia or a deeper understanding of the stresses of caregiving) has been accomplished through the portrayal.

As for Paul, I have operated all these years on an assumption of *implied* consent, for he suggested more than once that I write about our relationship. While I have revealed many details about his private life, I have done so with a larger purpose in mind, and I believe that Paul would approve. I have tried, in Couser's words, not to "override" his interests or "overwrite" his stories by imposing an "alien shape" on them that would be "gratuitously harmful" or that would suit my literary purposes while (if he were alive) rendering him unrecognizable to himself or, even worse, shocked at my characterizations. With these concerns in mind, Couser establishes the following "ideal standard" for the auto/biographer, which I agree with and have tried to follow: the writer should strive for a "justice of portrayal," in which the subject is portrayed as he would like to be seen and in a way that is in his best interests or the interests of those he represents.

Couser's standard is consistent with a feminist ethics of representation. As explained by the feminist ethnographer Kamala Visweswaran, portrayals of others (vulnerable or otherwise) are "ethical" if the author can answer the following questions positively: Will subjects recognize themselves in the account? Will they feel good about having developed a relationship with the writer? Will they feel that a greater good has been served by their involvement? As Visweswaran says, the issue is not merely how "good" the writing is, but whether the writer is "accountable to [others'] own struggles for self-representation and determination."[16] This is another way of saying that we owe respect and due recognition to others in our written accounts of them.

I believe I have met these ethical challenges. In the end, of course, I do not know how Paul or the other residents and staff members at Bedford Continuing Care would feel about my characterizations in *Endnotes*. I can only hope that they would recognize my purpose— to change how readers think and feel about old people—and believe that I had succeeded.

2 HOME

The old Bedford Nursing Home had an appealing facade. Although the building had always been a hospital of some sort, from the outside, it looked more like a stately home. Its two stories were built in the Georgian style, with red bricks, multipaned windows trimmed in white, and dormers in the slate roof. A veranda ran along the west side, easily accessible to patients seeking the afternoon sun. The grounds were parklike, with mature oak, maple, and pine trees on several acres of land.

In the 1920s, the Bedford was a children's hospital. Hundreds of kids with polio sought hydrotherapy here, and a world-famous surgeon transplanted cords and tendons to correct the deformities in their legs. After the discovery of the polio vaccine, the number of children needing a residential hospital decreased dramatically, and the state rented the facility to a series of agencies providing psychiatric treatment for disturbed children. In the late 1960s, the old Bedford was purchased and converted to a 179-bed private nursing home.

By 1996, the building itself was in a state of decline. The plumbing was bad, the roof leaked, and the old wards were too cold in the winter and too hot in the summer. After several months of deliberation, the board of directors decided to replace the building with a new complex to be called Bedford Continuing Care, reflecting changes during the 1980s and 1990s toward progressive care communities, which provided opportunities for residents over sixty-five to buy homes in an area where they could live independently yet take advantage of assisted-living services as needed. If their health declined further, they could move into a nursing facility on the same grounds.[1] The new Bedford facility would include a state-of-the-art nursing home, surrounded by condominiums. The new accommodations would be much more expensive, but all residents of the old Bedford would be grandfathered in under the current rates.

The director of nursing briefed me on the residents' feelings about the move, scheduled for September. Many longtime residents were having trouble with the prospects of leaving "home." They would miss their wardmates, their regular aides, their routines, and above all, the congenial atmosphere they had created in the public spaces of the old building. The new facility had much smaller spaces, and there would be no place for everyone to congregate on Friday nights to watch movies, a cherished ritual. The dining hall in the old Bedford was large enough to accommodate every resident. The new facility was designed to create a family-like dining experience, with small dining rooms on each wing. Residents who had brought furniture from home and tacked pictures up on the walls of the old Bedford would have to leave these things behind. The new building was fully furnished in carefully coordinated colors, complete with framed pictures that matched the decor. Residents who had toured the facility agreed that it was beautiful, modern, and efficient. But it felt like a hotel, not a home. As the facilitator of two writing group "interventions," my job was to encourage residents to talk and write about their fears and concerns about the move, as well as their curiosity

15

and excitement. It would be like group therapy without a therapist. Previous research on writing groups in nursing homes had determined that participants were less depressed and better able to communicate their thoughts and feelings.[2]

When I arrived at 9:00 a.m. on that July day to meet the residents for our first session, it was already oppressively hot. The morning group was to begin at 10:30, but I had a lot to do before then. The social worker had given me a list of people who had either volunteered or been "encouraged" to participate, but I knew only their names. I still had to determine who they were so that I could plan the session accordingly.

On my ride up to the second floor, I noticed a drawing with a caption on the elevator door. A crowd of people strained against a rope tied to a huge boulder. Underneath someone had penned the words, "Thirty days and counting. When we all pull together, we can do anything!"

I found the director of nursing in her cinderblock office, surrounded by boxes half full of files and papers. She was very busy, as nursing home administrators always are (even when not in the midst of a move), so we got right down to business. I called out the names on my list, while she looked at their medical charts, reading off abilities and disabilities and adding other details she thought might be relevant.

Mavis Atchley, early seventies, stroke patient. Used to be a bookkeeper in a nursing home. Often critical of Bedford.

Alice Billings, heart disease and arthritis. Lame in one leg and used a wheelchair. Still sharp, with a good sense of humor, but suffered occasional bouts of depression.

Camille Forest, ninety-eight, Bedford's oldest resident. Frail, with a long list of health problems, nearly deaf, but alert and sociable.

Eleanor Cohen, late sixties, multiple sclerosis. Chair of the Residents' Council, active and outspoken. Moved to Bedford twelve years ago when her husband died.

Constantine Kraja, serious heart problems, hospitalized twice this year. Very depressed since the death of his wife.

Paul Mason, early eighties, Parkinson's. Tremors and mobility problems, but "totally there." The "goodwill ambassador of Bedford."

Rose Atkins, late seventies, arthritis, heart and circulation problems. Has had trouble adjusting to institutional life.

Hester Wall, mid-eighties, Alzheimer's. Wanderer. Can't communicate much but enjoys social stimulation.

Ronald Gray, late fifties, cerebral palsy, confined to a wheelchair. Likes to talk but difficult to understand. Longtime resident of Bedford.

I left the director's office and made my way to the dining room, where our group was scheduled to meet. It was a large, echoey rectangle with high ceilings—woefully inadequate for interacting with a group of people who couldn't see, hear, or speak very well. On this morning, air conditioners blasted ineffectually from every window, making it impossible for even the able-bodied to hear above the roar. As the aides wheeled in residents, Shelly, the graduate student volunteer, and I moved tables around to form a conversation area. We introduced ourselves and made name tags, more for us than the group members, since many of them already knew each other. At the last possible moment, I switched off the air conditioners. We were immediately engulfed in sweltering air.

Even under the best conditions, the initial mood of a nursing home writing group is usually subdued. Here, as in every other home I had visited, residents operated with major sensory deficits that made communication difficult. Wheelchairs, too, put them at a greater social distance from each other. I stood amid the tables and chairs, speaking as loudly as possible without shouting.

I lay out the plan for the next four weeks and distributed a list of writing topics. At the beginning of each session, I would read aloud a short passage on the day's topic to get them thinking. Then the volunteers and I would move around and assist whoever needed help with their writing. At the end of each session, I would read aloud what everyone had written. I explained that I had learned this format from social workers who conducted writing groups in other nursing homes, and that it seemed to work well. Those who were unable to write could talk to the volunteers, who would take dictation.

Our topic that day, "my childhood home," generated quite a bit of interest. Alice, with Shelly's help, wrote about her father, a traveling salesman and a gambler, and her mother, whom he left alone to raise the children. Her mother bought coal on credit and baked pies to pay the bills. Rose, who wrote on her own in a flourishing hand, produced a full-page description of her mother's kitchen stove—a clunky, cast-iron monstrosity—in contrast to the parlor stove—a new, sleek, silver model that her mother kept polished to a sheen. Eleanor scribbled out three rapid-fire pages, describing how jealous she had been when her parents brought home a baby sister. Hannah remembered only that she had lived in New York City and that her mother had been a good cook. Paul recalled the noon whistle in the Michigan village where he had lived with his grandmother. Whenever she went to town, she would leave a plate lunch in the icebox for him. When the whistle sounded, he knew it was time to eat. "That whistle always sounded like picnic to me," Paul said. Camille remembered her grandmother's house, with the homemade lace curtains that had to be washed by hand and put on stretchers to dry. Horse-drawn carriages would zoom past the house and ride up on the curb as they turned the corner. Constantine summarized his entire life in two pages: kayaking on the river as a kid, joining the merchant marines, getting married, the death of his wife, and now, his own declining health. He informed us that he probably wouldn't be back next week, since he had already written everything important about his life. Ronald talked about his younger sisters and the duplex they had lived in on Twenty-third Street in Detroit. He got tears in his eyes when he described his stepmother, who had been too upset to visit when he first moved to Bedford. Ronald had known then that he would spend the rest of his life in a nursing home, and he had decided to make the best of the situation.

I read all of this aloud at the end of the hour, rushing over the last few. Everyone was getting restless from the heat, and the aides were already starting to wheel in the lunch crowd.

"Well, thank you, everyone, for coming and sharing your memories with us," I said in a wilted voice. "Next week, we'll talk about your first home-away-from home, when you got married, joined the service, or went off to school or work." An aide cranked up the air conditioners again, and the room was filled with a mechanical roar.

Paul Mason motored up to me in his battery-powered scooter and said, "What outfit are you with again?"

"Wayne State University," I responded.

"Well, you did a good job. That was very interesting," he said and spun away.

IN THE following weeks, Shelly and I circulated among the group members, getting to know everyone better. We arrived early each week to set up and assist the staff in getting residents to the dining room. When we came in the third week, we discovered that several aides were out, and everything was off schedule. At 10:25, only half the group members were seated in our little conversation area. I checked the roster to determine who was missing and headed for Paul Mason's room.

I met him in the corridor. It was the first time I had ever seen him standing, and it occurred to me that he didn't take up much space. He was a very small, quiet man.

"I'm walking today," Paul said. "I need the exercise, but I'm slow." He spoke softly and selected his words carefully, as if to conserve energy.

I offered my arm, and he put a thin hand on it. I noticed, too, that he walked much slower when he was talking. At one point, he stopped completely. "Move, dammit!" he said to his feet. "I have to remind myself to walk," he apologized. "It's Parkinson's."

"That's all right," I said. "Take your time." But I was feeling anxious about getting back to the group.

19

"I've had this cane for years," Paul said. "A friend of mine in South Carolina made it from a live oak root. See? The handle's in the shape of a duck's head. It provides a steady understanding."

"Very nice," I said, looking at the knobby black stick. I liked the way Paul oriented himself around small details. I had observed this in his writing, too; it set him apart from the other group members.

When we got to the dining room, Paul apologized for making me late. After my opening comments, I sat down next to Camille, who was sitting next to Paul. As we talked, I noticed out of the corner of my eye that Paul was looking distressed and had risen to leave.

"You're not going already, are you?" I asked.

"I forgot my glasses," Paul said. "I can't see a thing without them."

"But you'll miss the session if you have to walk all the way to your room and back."

"I guess this just isn't my day," Paul said, his voice faltering.

Ronald, who was sitting nearby in his motorized chair, offered to fetch Paul's glasses.

"Should I let him?" Paul asked.

"Yes, let's, since he's willing."

"They're on my dresser, Ronald," Paul said.

While he waited for his glasses, Paul closed his eyes and listened as Camille described the band concert she had attended the previous night on the Bedford lawn. She spoke in an almost ethereal voice about the balmy evening, the music, the company of her daughter. "When you hear music, especially outside on a beautiful evening, it's heavenly, it really is," Camille said breathlessly. "It was just the right time to hear it, too, after dinner."

"She's getting excited about her own memories," Paul murmured to himself.

By the time I had finished with Camille, Paul had his glasses on and was feeling more like himself.

"Who is that woman?" he asked, as I scooted my chair around to face him.

"That's Camille Forest."

"She seems like a very nice person."

"Yes, she is."

"I've had the benefit of knowing many good people in my life," Paul said. "My mother died in the great flu epidemic of 1918. They couldn't get her into the hospital fast enough, because all the beds were full. I watched them take her out the front door on a stretcher. It affected me deeply. I was five years old and the baby of the family. My grandmother had made a promise to my mother, and she was loyal to that. She took me into her home and treated me like her own. I called her Mama. After my grandfather died, it was just us two."

I nodded and wrote everything down.

"It was a delight to live there, and I liked to do what I could for my grandmother. She had a rusty old wringer-washer in the basement, and every time she went down the basement steps, she'd say, 'I'd sure like to get that thing out of here.' One day, when she was on one of her shopping trips to town, I figured out a way to move the washing machine. I wasn't even tall enough to see over the top of it, but I found a couple of board planks in the shed, and I rolled the washer over the planks, end over end, up the steps and out the back door. When Mama came home and saw it in the yard, she got all misty-eyed and said to my Aunt Martha, 'I *told* you he was the man of the house!'

"My aunts and uncles were good to me, too. My Uncle Bob was quite a character. There were some legal questions surrounding him, something about embezzlement, but I was too young to understand it. I didn't think my Uncle Bob liked me much, but he was smarter and more thoughtful than I knew at the time. One day I came home from school, and he and my grandmother and my aunt were standing in the middle of the sidewalk with a little bay pony. He'd brought it for *me*! He didn't say a thing, just watched my face. I'm sure I lit up like a firefly. I had that pony for four years, a chubby bay mare. Then I came home one day, and Uncle Bob had taken her away without an explanation, just the way he had brought her. I was one sad little boy.

But a year later, Uncle Bob came home with a malamute, a stray he had seen several times around town. He had watched the dog cross the street and was impressed at how smart and self-sufficient he was in traffic. So he brought him home to me. And it was true, he was one smart dog. He could ride a horse, just hang over the side like a sack of grain. All I had to say was, 'Leo, come on!' and he'd jump up and hang on. He seemed tickled to do it, too.ʺ

I was delighted by these stories, full of sensory details and memorable characters, and utterly charmed by the little boy Paul.

"Are you married?" Paul asked, as we finished writing.

"No, I'm not."

"How can that be, a beautiful girl like you?"

"Ah, well, a good man is hard to find, I guess."

"Yes, I imagine you're right," he said, looking at me closely. "You know, you're making me remember a lot of things."

"That's good, don't you think?"

"I suppose so," Paul said.

PAUL STOOD in the doorway of the dining room, leaning on his cane. I had already begun reading aloud a short story called "The Dining Room Table," about a woman who had decided to sell the table around which she had fed her many children, now grown and moved away. Some of the group members were wiping tears from their eyes.

"Hello, Paul," I said, nodding at him. "Come in and join us."

"I'm sorry I'm late," Paul said in his small voice. "Someone volunteered to cut my throat, and it took a while." He had a piece of toilet paper stuck to his neck. Paul made a forward motion, but his feet seemed to be glued to the floor. Shelly went over and gently nudged him toward a seat.

The day's topic was "transitions to new places," and we spent some time discussing the move, now only three weeks away. Group members were worried about whom they would have for roommates (they could choose, but many hadn't), what their rooms would be like, and whether their belongings would fit into the smaller spaces. They had been asked to clean out their closets and drawers and dispose of things they didn't absolutely need, a nearly impossible task for some. They had no choice about the location of their new rooms, which was a source of great concern.

"What if we don't like where they put us?" Eleanor said. "They're making that decision for us, and I would have liked to make it for myself, and others would, too. We're not senile, you know."

Even Camille, who always saw the positive side of things, was reluctant to leave her room in the old Bedford. "I have a very nice, cozy corridor," she said. "There's a window here and a window there. It's very pleasant. It makes me feel good in the morning when I wake up and ask the aide to open the blinds. When I look out the window, I see the sky and the top of the trees. To me, that's beautiful. I asked my daughter if I could see out the window of the new place. I don't think she knew how to answer. I'm in doubt. If something in life happens that you can't help, that's God's will. But I don't look forward it."

Alice was particularly emotional, sniffling during my reading of the short story and crying outright during our writing period. She had spent the previous day visiting her daughter and was feeling melancholy. The family had gone shopping at a local grocery store, where Alice was amazed to find a hole in the wall where you could put your plastic bottles for recycling. "Time has passed, and civilization has made some progress since I've been in here," she said. "I didn't want to come home from my daughter's. I wanted to stay overnight. I thought I was up to things, but my daughter didn't agree. I guess I don't have any patience any more. I'm getting old. I feel like I'm breaking down, and I get angry at having no self-control. Nobody can do anything about it. It's nobody's fault. Maybe I've been too lonesome, I don't know. They asked us to pick a partner. The lady in the office was really nice about it, but I haven't picked anybody yet. I like Victoria, who eats with me. There are quite a few people I've been with. I stop and say hello to people, but to pick someone, it's difficult. I really admire this lady Eleanor, who takes care of all the bingo."

Alice reached for a tissue. "What we just did, writing all that down, would cost me fifty dollars at a therapist's."

When I read aloud what they had all written, many nodded at Eleanor's final words: "I'm just taking it day to day. It has to be done, and I have to get used to it. It's hard for me, but I just have to do it. When I've had to deal with these kinds of things before, I dealt with it the same way—just work to hold it together. People have to pull themselves up to keep from feeling sad. After this hour, I'll go play cards. There are positive things, too."

Since this was our last session, I left time for them to evaluate the group experience. I had prepared a little survey, and the volunteers went around asking the questions: How satisfied were they, overall? Had they felt comfortable talking and writing? Would they do anything differently? Since we were short-handed, I sat down to help the nearest person complete the survey. It happened to be Paul.

"You sure are pretty," he said, as I pulled up a chair.

"Thank you," I said, getting down to business. "Now, we have this form to fill out. We'd like to know what you thought of the group sessions and how me might improve them."

Paul was silent for a moment. "You've got me way back in my childhood, thinking about dogs and ponies, and now I feel like you're pulling away, and I'm standing on the dock, waving goodbye."

"Oh," I said. "I can just see that little boy standing there all alone!" His sadness had caught me off guard.

"I'd like to continue with what I wrote," Paul said. "There's so much more to tell. It's like opening an old chest in the attic, and then closing it up tight, before you've taken everything out and examined it."

"Maybe I could—" but I stopped myself. I was thinking that someone needed to work with Paul individually, do an oral history or sit and write with him every day for a while. But I didn't want to make promises I couldn't keep. And there was the research project to think about. It would be inappropriate for me to spend extra time with him while the study was going on, and the researchers would be collecting data for the next couple of months.

"I'm sorry we couldn't stay longer," I said.

"I've enjoyed our time together," Paul said. "I'm sorry to see you go."

I returned two weeks later to distribute their writings, which I had typed and bound in spiral booklets titled "Reflections of Home." I had spent a lot of time putting these together, and I hoped the residents would like them. I was afraid some of them wouldn't even remember me, much less care about the booklet.

It took most of the morning to find everyone. They were scattered about the old Bedford, watching TV or napping in their rooms, getting their hair done in the beauty shop, exercising in the therapy room, playing a trivia game called "What Do You Remember?" with the activities director. Constantine and a woman from the afternoon group had been admitted to the hospital. Another woman from the afternoon group had been released and sent home. I passed by Paul's room several times, but I didn't see him. I finally found him at lunchtime in the dining hall.

"I've been looking for you all morning!" I said, taking a seat at the table.

"I'm a hard person to catch up with," he said, chuckling. His hair was tousled, and he looked as if he'd just gotten up from a nap. He was wearing a flannel shirt, despite the summer heat. When I took his hand, it was cool.

There was another man at the table who seemed to be in a trance.

"That's Morris," Paul said. "He can be very congenial, but he's having a bad day."

"I brought you this booklet," I said, pulling it out of my bag.

"Oh, that looks nice," Paul said warmly. "It's good to see you again. I've been thinking about all the letters I need to write to friends and family in South Carolina. All this correspondence. I feel bad that I haven't kept up with it."

"I'm sure people understand. Have you thought about tape-recording?"

"Yes, but I haven't done it. I can't find my tape recorder, for one thing."

I opened the book to the first page and showed Paul his name in the table of contents. My name was at the bottom of the page, along with the project staff and our university affiliation.

"I didn't know you were associated with the university," Paul said. "What do you do?"

"I'm an English professor. I spend a lot of my time doing research and writing."

"I just feel trapped here, like I'm in a cage. All the things I can't do, places I can't go. Do your writing while there's still time," he said with emphasis. He reached over and put his hand on top of mine. I found myself leaning down and rubbing my cheek gently over the top of his hand.

"Don't," Paul said. "Don't do that."

I didn't say anything.

"You don't know what I mean, do you?"

"No."

"I don't want you to go away wondering what I was talking about. I mean, don't look that way."

"What way is that?"

"Perfect. Just perfect. You are as pretty as I remembered."

I smiled.

"I love you," Paul said. He looked straight into my eyes.

"I love you, too," I said, looking right back at him.

The other man didn't seem to be paying attention.

"How are you getting around today?" I asked, surprised at myself and not knowing what else to say. "Can you carry this book back to your room, or shall I deliver it?"

"You could walk me back after lunch."

"That won't work," I said. "I have to talk to some other people."

"Oh," Paul said. He looked down at his hands. His nails were yellow and hadn't been trimmed in a while.

"Well, how long will lunch last?" I said, reconsidering.

"Three quarters of an hour or so."

"OK. I'll go see these other people and come back when I'm finished. If you haven't left by then, I'll walk you back."

"That will be fine."

When I returned half an hour later, Paul had already finished eating, and the other man had left.

"I'm ready," Paul said, picking up his cane. "Since your hands are clean, how about if you carry the book?"

"What'd you have for lunch?" I asked, as we inched our way through the dining hall.

"Liverwurst."

"I didn't know people still ate liverwurst," I said. "I'm a vegetarian myself."

"So if I asked you out for a steak dinner, you wouldn't go?"

"I'd eat the salad and the roll. And the dessert. I love dessert."

"It used to be that if you didn't buy a *steak* dinner, you were considered cheap."

"Yeah, well, it's maybe a little easier to date these days. A lot of women pay their own way."

"I can walk faster, you know," Paul said. "You're babying me." He began to speed up. "I could run to the end of the hall if I wanted to." He took three or four big strides.

"Hey, that's pretty good!" I said. "I didn't know you could do that."

Paul slowed down to his usual pace. "It's just that sometimes I fall into a deep exhaustion. Just fall into it. That's when I shuffle."

We passed his room.

"Shall we walk some more, Paul?"

"Yes, why not?"

27

We walked to the end of the hall and then back to his room. Paul tossed his cane into the corner with several others. "The woodpile," he joked.

"I apologize for this room," Paul said, surveying the clutter. "I'm not much of a decorator." He reached for the remote and turned the blaring TV down to a drone.

"I think it looks homey," I said.

"Homely is more like it."

"How'd you manage to get this room all to yourself?" I asked.

"I have no idea how I could be so lucky," Paul said. "Dan negotiated it. He never explained how he did it, but I'm grateful. We're trying for the same setup in the new place, but I haven't heard anything yet."

"Dan is your son?"

"Yes, and he's a good boy."

There was a single hospital bed in the corner next to the window, covered with a homemade afghan. Paul had brought his own dresser, the glass top of which was covered with items: a can of Barbasol shaving cream, Old Spice deodorant, a dusty bottle of nonalcoholic beer, a Detroit Tigers cap, piles of cards and letters, a fingernail filing kit. Several pictures were stuck around the edge of the mirror. Paul with a baby. A side shot of Paul wearing glasses and looking twenty years younger. A man with a graying beard holding the same baby. A collie dog. Paul and a silver-haired woman in an etched plastic frame that said "Aloha!" An older Paul, considerably depleted, in a baggy green sweatsuit, dancing with an aide. A portrait-size color photo, framed, of Paul and the silver-haired woman was centered on the wall next to the bed.

Across from the bed sat a 13-inch TV. Wedged between the wall and the bed, facing the TV, was a motorized recliner, the kind that tips the seat back to a recumbent position and forward to a standing position. A small lamp sat on a bedside table, along with some large-print Reader's Digests. In the corner next to the tangle of canes, Paul had parked his battery-powered scooter.

I peered at the pictures on the mirror. "Is this Dan?" I asked, pointing to the man with the graying beard. "He looks very kind."

"You've hit it right on the head," Paul said. "Dan is the kindest person you'd ever want to meet. He's a small businessman, just like his old man was. That's my grandson with him."

"Where's his wife?"

"I don't know. Her picture's around here somewhere—his second wife. This is his second family. The first one's pretty much grown up."

"My, you used to be much heavier, didn't you?" I said, surveying the picture of Paul and the silver-haired woman in Hawaiian shirts.

"Parkinson's. All that shaking makes you skinny."

"And this must be your wife?"

"That's my girl!" Paul said. "She was a teacher. When we retired, I wanted to take a mobile home and go all over the country. She didn't want to do it at first, but then she agreed. After we got home, she said, 'I'm glad you made me do that.'"

"She was a homebody sort of person?"

"Not exactly. She had traveled all over the world before I met her. China, Europe, Taiwan. Just when she got older . . ."

"How long has she been gone?"

"She died two years ago on my birthday, shortly before I moved in here."

"Oh, that must have been hard!"

Paul had been standing in front of me as we talked. I noticed that he was only a couple of inches taller than I, but he stooped a little. His left foot lifted up off the floor just the slightest bit as he leaned on his cane. He was wearing leather slippers with no socks.

And then he was standing next to me, one hand on my back. His fingers, cupped together, had landed in the middle of my spine, like a small bird come to rest for a moment on a branch.

"I guess I should be going," I said, clearing my throat.

"Do you have any more work to do here, now that the writing group is over?" Paul asked, keeping his hand in place.

29

"I'll be back in a month or so to conduct a follow-up meeting with the group members. We can talk then about how you might continue your writing, if you like."

"Yes, I've been thinking about what else I want to include," he said. "And how to make some continuity out of it."

"It's not often that I meet a fellow writer," I said. "You seem," I hesitated, "to have the soul of a poet."

"Be careful. You'll lift me right off the ground with those words," Paul said.

I kept my voice casual. "Anyway, I'm glad you were in the group. I'll miss seeing you each week."

"It was nice to be there," Paul said, dropping his hand. "Stop by whenever you're here."

"Thank you. I'll do that."

I walked out the door and took a few steps down the hall.

"Ruth?" Paul said quietly from the doorway.

I turned. It was the first time he had ever spoken my name. Paul met me in the hallway, and we walked toward the front door together.

"Hey, you're moving really well now!" I said. He was standing tall and striding forward.

"It takes effort and concentration, but I can do it sometimes," Paul said.

We passed the receptionist in the lobby, a stern-looking woman with a German accent. Paul gave her a friendly salute. Her eyes followed us to the door.

"Thank you for seeing me out," I said, turning to face him. He was standing very close. There was a light breeze coming through the screen door. Then he kissed me lightly on the lips. Without a second's thought, I returned the kiss.

As I walked across the parking lot in the shimmering heat, my brain took over. What on *earth* was I doing? But I couldn't stop smiling.

ONE BOY'S PARADISE:
PAUL'S RECOLLECTIONS OF CHILDHOOD

I used to write poetry. Here's a little ditty I wrote a while back. At least, I *think* I wrote it. I don't remember reading it anywhere:

How do I love thee?
Let me count the ways.
Now that there's computers,
It don't take so many days.

I didn't say that I was a *good* poet.

I could go on and on about my childhood. I was a happy, healthy little boy. I have my grandmother to thank for that. She made me feel loved and secure. I've carried that with me all my life.

I've always liked people, and they have usually liked me. I appreciate their little idiosyncrasies. What could be more interesting than people? Look around you, there's a joke a minute.

I had a good deal of freedom for a little boy, and I embraced it. My grandparents' property in Redford, which was a rural area then, was my home base, but I explored a wide radius around it.

I used to fly kites. I'd like to do that with Dan's boy now, if I could. A spring day that is breezy and bright is perfect for flying a kite.

One day, I was out in the yard, and my grandma called me in for supper. I didn't want to put my kites up just yet, so I tied the smaller one to the string of the larger one, and I tied the string of the larger one to a tough weed and went in for supper. Then we got busy with something in the house, and I just left those kites flying high all night long. The windows were open, and you could hear their gentle flapping. The wind never shifted, just a steady, uplifting breeze. Those kites were still flying in the morning. I could have gotten a Boy Scout medal for that, because I had made them myself. I knew all about nature and animals and making things from the materials at hand. Little boys just know how to do those things, somehow, or at least we did back then.

I had a good setup there on Berg Road. A big house and yard, an 18-hole golf course right across the road with the River Rouge running through it. And my grandparents. Two kind and quiet people to talk things over with.

When I got a little older, I worked at the golf course. I learned about people, improved my stroke, and got a lot of free balls in the deal. After work, I'd go off in the woods and hunt for balls. I had a pretty good idea where they were.

My grandma was my mentor. I called her Mama, and I loved her cooking. She was a simple cook, nothing fancy. I'd sit down at the kitchen table, rub my hands together and say, "Let's talk! But we need some warm biscuits and marmalade." And she'd produce them, out of nowhere, it seemed to me.

I had a teacher in elementary school whose name was Mr. Dimond. I was about the only one in the class who spelled it correctly, without an "a." I won a spelling bee in his class once. The word was "alcohol." When Mr. Dimond said it, there was a murmur in the room, because nobody thought anybody could spell it. But I knew the word because I'd seen it on cans around the house. My uncles were always dealing with alcohol—wood alcohol and green alcohol. I spelled it correctly, and everyone in the class congratulated me. I was a little embarrassed about all the fuss. I felt I had an unfair advantage.

When I was eight or nine, I had a little rabbit business, fifty-nine of them, to be exact. I kept them penned up, but every once in a while, I'd let them out to play in the yard, just run around and stretch their legs. Of course, they'd dart all over hell, run under the neighbor's fence and start eating out of his garden. He never said anything to me, but one day my grandma said, "Now, he's a nice man, and he likes you and doesn't want to hurt your feelings. But you've got to keep those rabbits out of his garden." And I thought, maybe it's time to give up the business. I decided right then. I put them all in a big box on top of my wagon, and I pulled it down the road to another neighbor's house who also had a rabbit business, only much larger than mine. He used to dress them out for customers and use the pelts for things. I said, "Here, you're my friend, and I want you to have these." I considered him my friend because we had talked now and then about rabbits. He thanked me and took them. I didn't feel bad. I knew it was time.

But I did like to have animals around. When I'd get a little money, I'd run to Mr. Purcell's feed store to see what he'd gotten in lately. I was likely to buy some chicks. Anytime Mr. Purcell saw me in town, he'd say, "Come on over, Buddy, and see what we got." He had Rhode Island Reds, New Hampshire Blues, nearly any kind of chicken you could want.

I read a book once by a scientist who experimented with birds, and I did an experiment of my own. I took a baby sparrow that had fallen out of a nest and put it in a cage with a female canary. She raised that sparrow like it was her own. When it was grown, I let it loose, but I followed it around. It roosted in the rafters of Mr. Purcell's store. I'd sit on the bench out front and watch the sparrow fly in and out. I always knew it by its rusty chirp—not a sparrow's call, but not the melodic line of a canary, either.

Years later, when I lived in South Carolina, we had a family of jenny wrens out on our back porch. It was warm back there. They built nests in some Easter baskets on a shelf above the washer and dryer. You know that colored Easter grass? They made a nice round bed for themselves and their babies. I tried to keep the door ajar for them all the time, but sometimes I would forget and close it after the dog. When that happened, the wrens would watch and wait for an opening. I would let Penny back in, and they would zoom through the door. Some of our friends used to say, "What do you want birds on your porch for? Aren't you afraid of mites and lice?" And I would tell them that birds are cleaner than we are. They take a bath with sand. I was happy to have them around.

3 MAKING OURSELVES UNDERSTOOD

It was a cold, rainy day in the middle of October when I returned to Bedford. The leaves were in full color around the nursing home, but the day was so dark and gray I barely noticed them. Inside the new facility, though, everything was bathed in florescent white. Automatic doors opened to a tastefully designed lobby with coordinated shades of burgundy and gray on the carpeted floors, and turquoise and mauve on the walls. Each of the resident's rooms was exactly the same: private bath with wheelchair access and shower seat; built-in dresser with recessed area for TV; two wide windows covered with white miniblinds; bedspreads with abstract patterns in mauve, burgundy, and turquoise; and a framed print in matching hues above the bed.

It was a little past 9:00 a.m., and the dining rooms had already cleared out from breakfast. I went to work on the third-floor dementia wing, leafing through residents' charts at the nurses' station. The university research team was behind in its data gathering, and I had offered to help. My task that day was to take notes on the health status, mood, and psychological adjustment of the study participants (members of the writing groups and comparable control groups) over the past two months. I had never seen a medical chart before, and I was curious to see what doctors and nurses recorded. The charts included not only diagnoses and treatments, care plans, and advance directives, but also notations on the daily fluctuations of a person's life—temperature and blood pressure, requests for aspirins and laxatives, showers taken and denied.

This was a closed floor, which meant that every time I wanted to go downstairs, I had to get someone to open the elevator with a key or punch in an access code at the door. So I stayed at the desk and worked all morning. Around lunchtime, I went to the staff lounge and grabbed some cheap sandwich cookies the research team had left for the aides to munch on as they completed our surveys. I returned to my station and continued taking notes as the noon meal progressed. The dementia unit buzzed with activity.

A woman at a table repeated, over and over in a distressed voice, "PickupthecherryjuiceIspilledandtheKleenex," in one, nonstop string of words. I looked at the floor and saw a tissue lying under some else's chair, but no juice.

An aide was trying to feed Hester, who had been in the morning writing group.

"I don't want that cabbage," Hester said.

"It's not cabbage," said the aide.

"I don't want it. Throw it out!"

"You don't have to eat it," the aide said calmly. "Would you like a sandwich?"

"I hate cabbage! Get it away! I'm going to eat just what's on my plate." Hester began shoving food off her plate onto the floor.

At a nearby table, a man talked to an aide as she pulled trays off the lunch cart.

"You know, I have no bone in my leg," he said. "It's completely gone."

"Your bone's still there, Frank. You're walkin' on it."

"Not a bone in my leg. It shattered into a million pieces."

The aide chuckled. "You're a trip, Frank. Drink your milk."

Meanwhile, a short, plump woman in a pink sweatshirt and baby blue sweatpants wandered the hallway in blue bunny slippers. Her face puckered, and she began to whimper. "I don't know where I am," she mumbled. "I don't know where to go." She stopped briefly and then took a few mincing steps forward. Then she stopped again and whimpered. "I don't know where I am. I don't know where to go."

A lanky man with white hair was sprawled out on the floor, tracing the large, Aztec pattern on the new carpet. He was trying to pick up the pieces he had traced.

An aide emerged from a room next to the nurses' station, pushing an angry-looking woman in a wheelchair. "When you see my son, tell him to put it right down here," the woman hollered, to no one in particular. "Right here where they can't get it. They've got me locked up in that room all day long!"

Shortly after lunch, I moved down to the first floor nurses' station, grateful for the change of scenery. I always found the drag and pull of daily life in a nursing home exhausting, but the chaotic dementia unit made me feel even worse. I was tired, anxious, and irritated all at once. Only a few dementia patients lived on the first floor, and they were quiet and stationary. If their illness progressed to a point where they wandered or became disruptive, they were moved to the third floor.

While I looked over the charts, a man came into the dining room. He approached a brown-haired women slumped in a wheelchair.

"Honey, open your eyes," an aide said to the woman. "You have a visitor."

The woman made no response other than a slight ticking noise, "tdddtdtdtdtdtdtdtddtd, tdtdtdtdtdtdtdtd, tdtddtdtdtdtdtd."

Another aide walked by and smiled. "Sounds like my one-year-old," she said to me.

The man, who was wearing a University of Wisconsin sweatshirt, sat down across from the woman. He was accompanied by a reddish brown toy poodle on a leash.

"Hi, Kay," he said to the woman. "I've got the Red Baron with me today."

"tdtdtdtdtdtdtdtd."

"Can you get her hair done?" he said to the aide, who was now standing at the nurses' station.

"Oh, you'd like her hair done?"

"Yeah, I think that would be nice," he said.

"Any special style?" she asked.

"Well, I don't know what they have."

You want a set or a permanent?"

"Uh, anything would be fine," the man said. "Just make her look nice."

After the aide left, the man and woman sat there, not saying anything. Then he noticed me sitting behind the desk.

"Poor Kay," he said.

"Is she your wife?" I asked, walking over to the table where he sat.

"Yes."

"Does she recognize you?"

The man shook his head. He gave the dog a little more leash.

"I just got back from a reunion at the University of Wisconsin. I wish I could tell Kay about it. I was in the Hall of Fame."

"For what sport?" I asked.

"Running. I ran with Jessie Owens. Do you remember him?"

"I once saw an old newsreel about him. You must have been very good."

"Came in third."

"Did you continue to run over the years?"

"Well, I'm eighty-two now, so I'm not running much these days. But I used to run quite a bit. I liked sports of all kinds."

I put my hand on Kay's chair and said, "What about you, Kay, did you like sports?"

Kay lifted up her head. "Yeah, yeah," she said.

"No, she didn't," the man said, shaking his head. "She doesn't know what she's saying."

LATE IN the afternoon, I went to visit Paul. He was on the second floor in room 201. His door was open, but I knocked lightly on the doorjamb. No one answered. The only thing I could see from the doorway was the built-in dresser and the end of the bed.

"Hello?" I called. "Paul?"

When he didn't reply, I took a few steps into the room.

Paul was lying in his recliner, slumped to the side, eyes half shut, pants unfastened. His shirt had been buttoned wrong, there was white fuzz on his chin, and he was barefoot. He looked thinner and frailer than I remembered.

"Hello, Paul," I said.

Paul opened his eyes. "I can't believe it."

"How are you?" I asked. I was standing at the foot of his chair, the left side of which was pushed up against the wall. On the other side of the chair was the bed. The room was small, and there was no place else to stand. I noticed, though, that it was a private room. I leaned forward and looked into his face.

"I've been better," Paul said.

"I've seen you better," I said. "Have you been sick?"

"Yes, well—I've been ill, not sick. That's what I've been saying to everyone. It just hit me, this lethargy."

"I'm glad to see you sitting up and not lying in bed, at least," I said.

"I've been wondering how to get a hold of you," Paul said. "I have a list in my mind of people I want to see again, and you're on it."

"I'm flattered."

"Come over here," Paul said, motioning to the small space between the chair and the bed.

I moved the bed tray aside and inched myself into the space. Paul reached his arm up to me, and I learned forward to meet him. One, two, three little kisses. Paul's lips were trembling.

"Well, I'll be damned," Paul said.

"I don't think I'm supposed to sit on your bed," I said, surveying the room for a chair. "It's probably against regulations or something, but there's no place else to sit." I perched tentatively on the edge of the bed. Paul continued to recline in his chair, but took both my hands in his.

"Your hands are cold," he said.

"Yes. I've had chronically cold hands and feet since I was a kid."

"Hmm. I have reliably warm hands."

"So, what is this illness?"

"I don't know. These thoughts and feelings came over me. I've tried to work through them, but it takes time. I've thought about you often. About the last time we met, and I kissed you at the door. As I watched you walk away, I was saying to myself, 'You old fool.'"

"I feel strongly about you, too, Paul. Don't judge your feelings too harshly."

"There's so much to say. I'm an old man in a hurry, but I don't want to waste words. I don't understand what I'm feeling. It's strange."

"I don't understand it, either. But I'm trying to follow my feelings and see where they lead. It's something I haven't been very good at in the past."

"I've pretty much lived my life following my feelings. Does it— whatever is happening between us—make you sad?"

"No," I said. "Does it make *you* sad?"

"No. But I don't know how to think about it, what it means."

"Maybe it's not for us to understand. Maybe it doesn't mean anything. Maybe it just is."

"The way you are, the way you think, you're a very special person," Paul said. "That was just the right thing to say."

He pulled me toward him again. We kissed—one, two, three—and then another kiss, which Paul held longer. I pulled away.

"Paul," I said. "I'm here in a professional capacity. I can't spend more time with you than the other residents, at least until the study is over."

"What is the study?" Paul asked.

"Has someone from the university come in the past week and asked you questions?"

"Yes."

"That's part of the study."

"What are they doing with the answers?"

"Oh, putting them in the computer and looking for numerical patterns. We're wondering if there have been changes in people's moods and attitudes since the move."

"Ohh," Paul said, as if he thought it was a good idea. "How long will the study run?"

"Until December. They'll ask you the same questions again, and after that, it will be over. Until then, I can't spend time with you."

"I've taken you out for four or five steak dinners over the last few weeks," Paul said.

"Oh, yeah? You forgot I was a vegetarian?"

"Yes, I did. I can't think of where else to take you."

"Take me out for a seafood dinner. I still eat fish."

"Good. Maybe your hands would warm up if you ate red meat."

I laughed.

"I also took a trailer trip last week to Northern Michigan," Paul said. "You were with me."

"I would have liked that."

"Do you like music?" Paul asked.

"Yes, very much. I took years of piano lessons, and I played the clarinet in the band. First chair—well, sometimes."

"I've been wanting to see—what's the name of that musical they're advertising on TV? In downtown Detroit?"

"At the Masonic Temple? *Phantom of the Opera*? Funny you should mention that. I saw it last night with my mother."

"How was it?"

"Moving. Uplifting. Despite the fact that it's a tragic romance."

"There's so much to say, and I don't know how to say it right. I'm an old man whose mind is moving fast. Is there someone in your life I'm aggravating?"

"No, there's no one."

"It must sound arrogant to say I could aggravate anyone. But if there *were* someone, it wouldn't matter. I'd ignore him." Paul reached up and pulled me toward him. We kissed again.

"Thought I'd take one more crack at that professionalism," Paul said with a grin. We kissed again, lingering this time.

"Who are you?" Paul said. It was almost a groan. Then he lightened the mood. "You have five minutes to tell me your life story."

"What do you want to know?" I asked.

"Everything."

"I was born in a small town in Michigan in 1954. I have a twin brother, an older brother, and an older sister who's also my best friend."

"A twin?" Paul said. "I had twins. Dan's sister died, though. She smoked, and I used to beg her to quit. She said, 'It's my only fault, and I enjoy it, so let me smoke.' She died of cancer."

After a brief pause, Paul said, "How much do you weigh?"

"Geesh, Paul," I hesitated. "I weigh around 140, usually more than less, and I'm about five, seven. I always think I need to lose a few pounds."

"These details are important."

"I also like to dance," I said. "And I'm a pretty good ballroom dancer, if I do say so myself, although it's hard to find partners."

"I was a very good dancer, too. I could glide across the floor."

"I would have guessed that. It takes a certain kind of sensitivity to dance with a partner. You have to respond to the music and the other person, as well."

"You're right. That's why dancing is so romantic."

"When we go out for that seafood dinner, let's go dancing afterward," I said.

"Well, to be realistic—well, maybe I could. I might be able to dance for fifteen minutes or so. I'm old, you know. A hundred years old."

"How old are you, really? I don't think I ever knew for sure."

"Eighty-two. Born in 1914." Paul wiped his mouth. "My mouth is so dry. It's the medication, plus nervousness. Would you hand me that cup?"

I passed him the Styrofoam cup of ice water from the tray table. He drank it from a straw.

"You know, you have me at a disadvantage," Paul said, leaning back.

"Yes, I know."

"I'm sorry I look so awful and my mouth is so dry. I haven't shaved. I can't find my razor. It just disappeared. Next time you come, I'll be in better shape."

"You don't have to apologize, Paul."

"I'm a treasure, really. That's what Lila used to say. A man from the old school, with old-fashioned manners."

"Yes, I know that, too. That's one of the things I like about you."

"I think you're a treasure, too," Paul said. "We seem to have found each other at a most unusual time."

"I suppose so."

"Or maybe you're a spook—from somewhere that isn't real."

I laughed. "No, I'm here."

"I told my son about you," Paul said.

"Uh-oh. What did you say?"

Paul grinned. "That you were one damn good-looking woman. We have a close relationship, like two guys. I was going on and on about you, and then I thought I'd said too much, so I shut up."

"I hope you'll be discrete when you talk about us, Paul. People will think this is strange. Your son might worry."

"I will be discrete," Paul said. He reached up again, and we kissed. Paul tried to prolong the kisses, opening his mouth wider, but I pulled away. He traced my face with his finger.

"What a dish!" he said.

"We mustn't do this," I said. "The aide will be coming in. It could be embarrassing for both of us."

"I thought about your professional status before," Paul said. "But then I said to myself, I'll let God take care of that, and I'll take care of my part."

"I admire your courage," I said. "And your honesty."

We looked at each other. A voice called my name from the hallway. It was Shelly, the graduate research assistant.

"I have to go now, Paul."

He struggled to rise from the chair.

"Don't get up."

"I want to walk you to the door," Paul said.

"I know, but you've been ill. Relax."

"The last time you were here, when you came into the dining room, how did I look when I saw you?" Paul asked.

"A little surprised, I guess. Taken aback."

"I want you to know how I feel. My head was spinning. I felt as if I would faint from the surprise and the pleasure of it."

"I couldn't tell. You have a very polished demeanor. You were gracious and gentlemanly."

"Thank you," Paul said. "Now you know how I really felt."

I smiled at him. "Goodbye, Paul."

"Come back to me, my darling."

I RETURNED in late November to meet with the writing groups one last time. I wanted to hear what they thought about life in the new building.

Camille was already seated in the dining room.

"It's good to see you, Camille," I said. "I heard that you weren't feeling well and might not be here."

"Oh, hello, my dear," Camille said. "Yes, I've been so very ill. To tell you the truth, I'm halfway to death. You have such a sweet face."

"Thank you, and so do you."

"It's so good to see you. May I kiss you on the cheek?" Camille took off her glasses, and I leaned down.

"Oh, your skin is so soft!" Camille said. She began to stroke my hand. "The skin on your hand is soft, too! Just like mine used to be."

I laughed. Camille could find something to appreciate in just about anything.

"I've been in so much pain," Camille said softly. "All I can do is pray to God to take it away, and he does take some of it. I'll tell you, it feels like I'm sitting on three sharp spikes." She held up three bent fingers. "It's in my rectal area. I could show you."

"No, you needn't do that, Camille," I said hastily. "Have you spoken to the nurse about it?"

"Not today," Camille said. "I suppose I should say something. It's like three sharp spikes sticking into me. Maybe if I lift myself up out of my chair, you could see."

"I think you should talk to the nurse."

"I could forget," Camille said. "After lunch, I get sleepy and take a nap, and then I forget."

Just then, Paul appeared at the door, shaved and nicely dressed in a white shirt and khaki pants.

"My, you're looking much better than the last time I saw you," I said in greeting.

"I'm feeling much better," Paul said, smiling.

I discovered that the group members were variously pleased and disgruntled with the new surroundings. Those in wheelchairs complained that the dresser drawers were too deep to get their hands into. Some people didn't like their roommates. Favorite aides had been assigned to other residents, and there were new staff members to get used to. The beauty shop wouldn't be open for another year, which meant the women had to wash their hair in the shower. But they did like the decor and the central air and heat.

After I'd met with both groups, I went around to Paul's room.

He rose from the chair, took my hand, and kissed it.

"I've missed you," he said. "I thought about calling you several times, but then I thought about the professionalism, and I didn't."

"I appreciate that. But it's all right to call now. The study is pretty much over."

Paul gestured that I was to sit on the bed, while he took the recliner.

"I have just beckoned you to my bed," he said.

"Don't start, Paul."

"I'm not starting anything," he said cheerfully. "This has been going on since the beginning of time."

"Do you mind if we turn down the TV?" I said. "I can't hear you very well."

Paul took the remote control and pressed a button, which produced loud static. He hit another button, which changed the channel. Finally, he found the power button. "There," he said. "Now we can talk."

"How have you been?" I asked.

"Not bad, although I've had this shaky spell for a while now. I wish I'd get over it. My son takes me to the doctor, and the doctor is busy and doesn't know what's wrong and can't change anything anyway. He says, 'We have many others to take care of,' as if I'm taking up his time. My son goes into a room and talks to the doctor alone, like I'm not there at all. Your family does that when you get old. I talked to him about it once, but he's forgotten. There's nothing wrong, really, just feelings. You know about feelings?"

"Yes, I know about feelings."

"This is feelings," Paul said, reaching for my face with both hands. We kissed several times, gently, on the lips. He smelled of aftershave, applied sparingly.

"I love tenderness," Paul said.

"Me too," I said.

"I've had some trouble since you were here last," Paul said. "Someone stole my credit card. Took it right off the dresser. They proceeded directly to Hudson's and ran up a bill to the tune of $5,000. I'm not responsible for the debt, but the credit card company acted like it was a trifling amount—$5,400, to be exact."[1]

"Oh, that's awful!" I said. "It must feel like a terrible violation."

"Yes, it does. That's exactly how it feels."

"What is the administration doing about it?"

Paul shrugged. "Nobody tells me anything. I don't believe they've done a thing. It's very upsetting. Now I don't know who I can trust."

I didn't know what to say.

Paul drew my face toward him, and we shared several more kisses. Then I pulled away, leaving him in a pose of yearning.

"I have to go," I said quietly.

"The saddest words in the world," Paul said. "Where will you go after you leave? What will you do tonight?"

"I am going to get a haircut. And then I will go home to feed my cats."

"You have cats?" Paul said brightly. "I have a dog named Penny. I left her with Dan when I moved in here. She's a wiry little thing with big, understanding eyes and a wonderful personality. My son's wife doesn't like dogs, and I feel bad, like I let Penny down. When I visit her, she gets ecstatic. She's beside herself with excitement. It's quite a compliment." Paul chuckled at the thought of Penny leaping around his feet.

"I've always had a soft spot for men who like animals," I said.

"Where is that spot?" Paul said. "Can I move in? Put me in a corner right next to your heart, and I'll curl up there."

"You are utterly charming, Paul. But I have to go. My research assistant will be looking for me. She will know to look here, because she suspects that I like you. She doesn't know how much I like you, though."

"I don't think *you* know how much you like me," Paul said.

"Perhaps not," I said. As I rose to leave, Paul rose too, and we embraced. A surge of sexual energy passed between us.

"Call if you want to talk," I said.

"I can't. It would make me ache."

We embraced again at the door.

"Can I help you with anything?" Paul asked politely.

"No, I just have to get my briefcase and coat from the staff room, and I'll be on my way." We walked out into the brightly lit hallway, holding hands. We stood by the elevator, looking at each other.

"Why aren't you going?" Paul said, squeezing my hand.

"You have a strong grip," I said.

TWO WEEKS later, on a Friday night, my telephone rang.

"Hello?"

"What is he doing, bothering her at home like this?" said a low voice.

I recognized Paul's voice immediately, but it was an unusual opening line. "Who is this?" I said.

"Paul."

"Paul! What a surprise!"

I felt happy and confused at the same time. We talked for maybe fifteen minutes, with Paul apologizing periodically for bothering me.

"You were watching TV. I shouldn't keep you from your show."

"I can watch TV anytime."

"I thought about calling you at your office, but I didn't know who would answer or what they would think, and I didn't want to bother you at work."

"You wouldn't be bothering me, Paul. Call any time. If I'm busy, I'll call you back."

"I've been thinking a lot about you. I wondered if you'd forgotten me. When will you be coming back?"

"Late December."

"Late December! That seems like months away! Will you be able to visit more when you come then?"

"Yes. All the data will have been gathered and analyzed, and we can spend more time together if you want."

"Good. I'd like that. Tell me what you've been doing."

"I went to a conference in Boston, where I gave a paper on feminist gerontology to a huge audience that included Betty Friedan. I got a research grant to support my work in another nursing home, and the University of Virginia Press wants to publish my book."

"Holy cow! You've been busy. I'm proud of you."

"Thank you."

"And what are you doing right now?" Paul asked.

"Sitting on my couch, watching television."

"Are you alone?"

"No. One cat is sitting on my lap, and the other one is lying in the chair next to the couch. If you listen hard, you can hear the one in my lap purring."

"What does she look like?"

"She's a long-haired Persian, calico colored."

"What does the other one look like?"

"She's a tortoise shell, with an orange, black, and beige coat. Her face is split in half, black on one side and beige on the other."

"What a pleasant domestic scene," Paul said genially. "I'm happy to be a part of it, if only by phone."

"Yes, we like it here in our little house. I would be very lonely if it weren't for my cats."

"It's been a joy thinking about you all these weeks. But I'm as rambunctious as a young kid."

"That's good, right?"

"Yes, it's good. But—" Paul's voice faltered. "This is awkward. You are—very desirable."

"Thank you," I said, pleased beyond all reason. "I'll see you soon."

WHEN I returned to Bedford later that month, I had not seen Paul in six weeks. We had not spoken since our telephone conversation three weeks earlier. I was not sure how I felt about seeing him again. Part of me wanted to let the whole thing slide into oblivion. The other part was wildly curious about what was going to happen next.

It was noontime, and I headed for the south dining room on the second floor. Paul was sitting at a table in the corner with another man and a woman.

"Hi there," I said. "Mind if I join you?"

"Please do," Paul said. Neither one of us could stop grinning.

Paul introduced me again to Morris, who had been at the table the other time we met in the dining room, and his wife, Bea. Bea was feeding Morris small spoonfuls of macaroni and cheese.

"How've you been?" I asked Paul.

"Not bad, and you?" Paul said.

"Good, very good. I've missed you."

"I've missed you, too. I wasn't sure you'd stop and see me today. I heard you were in the building."

"Of course I'd stop and see you. I wouldn't miss it."

Paul sawed on a piece of Salisbury steak as we talked. He was trembling a little more than usual. He buttered a piece of bread and took a long time placing the knife back onto his plate.

"See, that's what happens with Parkinson's," Paul said. "I can't let go of it." He made a deliberate push to release the knife.

"I'm still annoyed about my credit card," Paul continued. "They never found it, but I got a statement from the credit card company that said, 'Fraud,' and I didn't owe anything. Those companies make so much money, they don't even blink an eye at the loss of $5,000."

"Did the nursing home ever investigate that theft?" I asked.

Paul shook his head. "They don't seem to care either."

"Well, that doesn't make *you* feel any better, does it?"

"To know that someone around here took it right off my dresser—"

Bea gave Morris some applesauce and ran the spoon over his mouth to catch the dribbles.

"Do you want something to eat?" Paul asked.

"No, thank you. I'll just sit here and watch you eat," I said.

"That's no fun," Paul said.

"I don't want to take your food. You need all you can get. Besides, I don't eat meat."

"Want some cranberry juice?"

I looked at the carton. "No thanks. It's actually fruit punch."

"My son doesn't eat meat, either," Bea said. "He had a heart attack last year and completely changed his diet. No fat, no cholesterol. He's very strict about it. He's only fifty-five."

I looked at the dietary card on Paul's tray.

"What's this?" I said. "Under 'dislikes' it says carrots, cabbage, and pineapple. You don't like carrots?"

"There's a story about that," Paul said. "I *do* like carrots, and cabbage, too. When I came here, they interviewed me about my food preferences. I had just had some dental work done, and I said I couldn't eat raw carrots or cabbage. They wrote that down, and I haven't seen a carrot since."

Bea picked up the card on Morris's tray and studied it.

"Here, take this banana," Paul said. "You've got to eat something, and I don't want it."

"OK, I'll save it for later."

"The best thing about this meal is dessert," Paul said, picking up a small carton of chocolate ice cream. "Do you like ice cream?"

"I love it, especially chocolate. But I don't allow myself to eat it much any more. I gain weight pretty easily these days."

"Have some," Paul said, dipping his spoon in the cup and holding it out to me. I leaned forward, and he began to feed me.

"Good aim," I said. "Next bite is yours."

We finished the ice cream as all the women around us watched. When we were leaving, Eleanor Kroner, who sat at the next table, said to Paul, "Is that your daughter?"

"Ha-ha, yeah, my daughter," Paul joked. "No, really, she's my niece." Paul moved on to speak to a woman at another table.

"Are you really Paul's daughter?" Eleanor asked me.

"No," I smiled. "You know how he likes to kid around. We're friends."

"I didn't think so," Eleanor said. "He's a nice man, don't you think? Very charming and debonair."

"Yes. Debonair. That's a good word for Paul. There aren't many men in my generation that I would call debonair."

"Believe me, there aren't many in my generation, either," Eleanor said.

Paul and I passed through the dining room and walked down the hall together. He turned and started to enter a room on the right.

"Where are you going, Paul? Are you planning to visit T. Winslow or J. McDonald?" I asked, reading the nameplates on the wall.

"Oh," he said. "I was going toward the TV noise, thinking it was mine."

"You're still down the hall a ways," I said, taking his arm.

When we got back to Room 201, Paul folded me into his arms, right in front of the door. Then we moved toward his recliner, and he pulled me toward him, kissing me several times.

"Can you find a way to get in here with me?" Paul said.

I laughed and tried to keep my balance, half standing and half leaning over Paul's chair.

"This is a little weird, don't you think?" I said.

"Yes, but in a good way. It's wonderful to see you. I've been trying to figure how I could take you out. My son has all my money. I have thirty cents on my dresser. Do you know any thirty-cent women?"

"Yeah, me. You don't have to buy my affections."

"But I'd like to take you out. I need to ask Dan for some bucks."

"What are you going to say?"

"Can I have fifty bucks?"

"I mean, what are you going to tell him you need it for?"

"To take a beautiful woman to dinner."

"How do you think he'll react?"

"If I know Dan, he'll say, 'Good God! When are you going to *stop*?!' Paul grinned. "I'll tell you something. No, I don't want to tell you that."

"What?"

"Several ladies were around me in the dining room the other day, joking and making innuendos, and I said, 'Ladies, I have never wanted to be intimate with a woman I didn't love.' They went gaga over that."

"You know what women like to hear, don't you? Have you always been a ladies' man?"

"Oh, no. I was a grandma's boy. I don't ask for all this attention, believe me."

"So, I have some competition, eh?" I asked.

"None. Not one woman around here or anyplace else could hold a candle to you."

We resumed our kissing.

After a while, Paul said, "Tell me something about yourself."

"What do you want to know? I'm an open book."

"I sensed that."

"What's the one thing you'd like to know most?" I asked.

"Who is he? The man you think about, the man in your life."

"I told you, there is no man in my life. I broke off a relationship about this time last year. There's been no one since."

"How long did it last?" Paul asked.

"Three and a half years."

"What happened?"

"He was a recovering alcoholic who started drinking again. He had several relapses over the course of a year. It destroyed our relationship."

"Foolish, to choose alcohol over a good woman. What could he have been thinking?"

"I don't think alcoholism allows much time for rational thought," I said. "He was a good man. I still loved him when I left."

"Then I rushed in," Paul said.

"Yes. I wasn't planning on it. I was married for seven years before that. I've been divorced about five years."

"How did that end?" Paul said.

"He decided he wanted to date other women while he was still married to me."

"How could a man want other women when he has a walking angel at home?"

"I don't think *he* saw it that way. I had waited a long time to get married. I was twenty-nine. I probably should have stayed single. It seems to suit me."

"No children?" Paul asked.

"Never wanted any."

"The same thing happened to me with my second wife, Joan. She said, 'You want me to have fun, don't you?' I said, 'Yes' and divorced her. Then I married Lila. When I was young, the guys I knew would say, 'Let's go out and tie one on and have some fun,' and even then, I would say, 'You crazy fools, you have a nice wife and kids at home. What do you want to do that for?' But still, I'm no angel."

We searched for words to describe our feelings.

"I've been way out there for some time—way far away—and now I'm coming back," Paul said. "I have enough love for three people, and I want to give it all to you. But I don't know how to make myself worthy of your love."

"Be honest with me about everything, all the time," I said. "Tell me exactly what you're thinking and feeling."

"I can do that," Paul said. "But there must be more."

"Be a good and kind person."

"I don't have to go into training for that."

"And care about who I am as a person, what my interests are, the things I care about."

"I want to know all about that."

"Well, then, that's it. Be exactly who you are."

"What about my slowness?" Paul said. "Does it, will it frustrate you, how slow I am?"

"That's part of your illness. Why should I be frustrated? We'll work around it."

"You're an incredible woman."

"Thank you. You're an incredible man."

"There's more," Paul said. "But I'm not going to tell you all of it at once."

"Going to parcel it out a little at a time?"

"Precisely. To keep you coming back."

I found Paul very easy to talk to. This was unusual, given my previous experiences with men my age who seemed always to be hiding something, or hiding *from* something.[2]

"I understand that you don't want to be embarrassed, and I agree," Paul said. "I understand that you don't want to be married, and I agree. I understand that you will go your way, and I will go mine, and I agree. I would just like to be close to the person I love."

"Good," I said. "We agree on the important things. But I need time to get used to these feelings. Let's take it slow. Do you know what I mean?"

"Yes, not fast," Paul said.

"You are such a smart aleck!"

Someone knocked on the open door. I leapt off the arm of Paul's chair and composed myself.

"Time for your Sinemet," said the nurse, rounding the corner of Paul's room. She hadn't waited for an invitation to enter.

"Ah, my medicine," Paul said. "You can see I'm a little shaky."

The nurse offered water and two red pills.

"Have a nice visit," she said on her way out.

A minute later, she returned. "Just looking for my pen. I seem to have left it somewhere," she said, scanning the floor around Paul's chair. When she didn't find it, she left.

"The old pen-drop scam," Paul said conspiratorially. We both laughed.

"My work here is done, so we can see each other more," I said.

"That's good."

"I thought, if you wanted to, we could write more of your life story," I suggested.

"I'm more interested in working on *this* chapter at the moment, but that would give us a good excuse to see each other, wouldn't it?"

"Yes, it would."

"Coincidences," Paul said. "So many coincidences in life. I have a lot of time to think about such things. I think I had to be older to recognize you."

"Maybe so."

"I'd like to write some of this down, the way things work out. I was thinking the other day about catastrophes in my life and how they changed everything afterward. The first was my mother's death. You may be in this story, too."

"Not as a catastrophe, I hope."

"Quite the contrary," he said. "I love you. I'm going to say that a lot. You'll probably get tired of hearing it." My hand was resting on the arm of his chair. Paul's right hand was extended rigidly over the top of mine. He was shaking a little.

"Shall we begin to work on that life story, then?" I asked. "How about next Thursday afternoon?"

"Any day, all day," Paul said. "I am here. I want to see you any time."

"OK, then. Thursday, it is. If you don't feel well, call me, and we'll reschedule."

"And you do the same, OK?" Paul said. He pulled my hand toward him, and we embraced in the chair.

Paul walked me to the elevator and whispered "I love you" as the doors closed. I sank against the elevator wall, weak in the knees. I said a silent prayer: Please don't let me do anything I'll regret later.

That night at home, I fell asleep on the couch. I awoke in the middle of the night, an alarm sounding in my head. A frightened voice said, "What are you doing? You are getting into something you will have a hard time getting out of! This is not a game. Stop this right now, before things go too far!" But another, quieter part of me was already thinking about seeing him again.

4 NEW YEAR'S EVE

Our first real date was the Bedford New Year's Eve party, which was held at two o'clock on the afternoon of December 31, 1996. What distinguished this party from all the other celebrations at Bedford was the fact that outsiders were coming, and there would be a toast with sparkling grape juice.

Paul had invited me three days earlier over the phone. I had already made tentative plans to go dancing with Steve, an ex-boyfriend, but Paul talked me out of it.

"I just assumed you and I would plan something," Paul said. "But I shouldn't have taken that for granted. Now I'm worried."

"Why? Steve and I used to take dance lessons together. We're old friends."

"Dancing can be very intimate, you know, and any man in his right-thinking mind would want more with you than friendship. I don't like this one bit, although I admit to being prejudiced against him. Is there anyone else like him lurking in the background?"

"No."

"Are you sure?"

"Yes."

"You'd better be sure. I can't think of anything harder than what we're doing right now. I'm glad you told me."

"I'll call and tell him I've made other plans. We hadn't finalized anything yet anyway."

"Why don't you let me call him?" Paul offered. "I'll say, 'Stevie boy, it's all over, kid.' He'll find somebody else, although she won't be of the same caliber."

"I'll call him this afternoon. It's not a big deal, Paul."

"He'll probably try to talk you out of it. He might want to see you in person. Just keep it light: 'I thought I'd tell you now, while there's still time to get another date. The field's wide open.' That kind of thing."

This made me laugh. I couldn't imagine myself saying, "The field's wide open."

"Call me right after you talk to him, will you? I want to know how it went. I hope I haven't talked you into anything. You won't feel guilty or depressed, will you?"

These old boyfriends had a tendency to crop up in our conversation from time to time. A couple of months later, I told Paul that Steve had called for a letter of recommendation. He was applying for a new job and wanted a character reference.

"A job recommendation!" Paul huffed. "Boy, they'll find a way, won't they? Is he going to come to your house to pick it up?"

"I guess so. He needs it soon."

"Slip it under the door and then lock it fast," Paul said.

For the next few days, Paul would ask about Steve, but not by name. "Did hurly-gurley pick up that paper?" "Have you seen Klem Kadiddle Hopper?" "Did flibbertigibbets come over yet? Yes? Did he try to kiss you goodbye? NO? That just goes to show you how silly he is."

For our New Year's Eve date, Paul met me around 11:30 a.m. at the elevator. We were going to have lunch together before the party. He was sitting in his wheelchair, wearing argyle socks under his slipper shoes. He was also wearing a belt. His nails were trimmed, and his white hair looked newly washed. I had never seen him so dressed up.

"It seems like I've been waiting forever," Paul said, as I stepped into the hallway. "The aides keep urging me to get down to the dining hall, and I keep saying, 'No, I'm waiting for my friend.'" He took my hand with a gracious air and kissed it. "Do you mind pushing me? I'm conserving my energy."

As we wheeled toward the dining room, Paul described his day so far.

"I was supposed to be all ready, but the screen on my electric razor broke. Lacerates my face. I called Dan to tell him I needed a new one. He said, 'I suppose you want to get it fixed before Ruth comes.' I said, 'Well, yes, ideally, but she's coming soon.'"

Paul was the only man I had ever met who recounted his daily life, including thoughts and feelings, in such detail. I liked that. It made me feel closer to him.

"I told Dan I don't know what you want with someone like me," Paul continued. "Well, I didn't use that language, exactly. I said, 'What's she want with an old fart like me?' And Dan said, 'Dad, you're a very special person.'"

"And he's right, too," I said, kissing the top of Paul's head.

"He's never said anything like that before. It made me feel really good."

Lunch had been scheduled earlier than usual so the aides would have time to prepare the dining room. The Bedford Bell Ringers were scheduled to perform promptly at 2:00 p.m. with a medley of their favorite tunes. As usual, Morris was already at the table when we arrived. He was having a good day and wanted to talk

"Mmmmmmmmmmmibelllrinnnnngggger," Morris stammered in his low voice.

"I didn't get that, Morris," I said. "You'll have to go slower."

"MmmmmmmmmIusedtobeabellringer."

"No kidding! Which note did you play?"

Morris paused and looked sideways. "I-ddddon't-remember," he said, haltingly. "The bbbbottom."

"Ohh, one of those low tones," I said suggestively and winked at him. Paul beamed.

Meanwhile, two aides stood to one side of the dining room, looking our way. "He got hisself a friend," one of them said in a clearly audible voice.

"They're talking about you," I whispered to Paul.

Paul mustered up his loudest voice and called across the room, "Careful, I hear pretty good." The young women giggled and turned away.

We finished lunch as quickly as possible and went back to Paul's room.

"Should I wear a jacket?" Paul asked.

"If you feel like it," I said.

"But would you *like* me to wear a jacket?"

"Well, yes, if you put it that way. You would look very handsome in a jacket."

"That's more like it," Paul said. "Now, which one?"

Paul laid three sport coats on the bed. I selected the blue ultrasuede.

"Excellent choice," Paul said, as I helped him into his coat. "I'm courting you, you know, and I want to look good."

We decided to walk back down to the party and pick up Morris on the way. Paul extracted his duck's head cane from the woodpile and offered his left arm to me.

As we entered Morris's room, he wheeled up to his closet and started stirring the clothes around.

"What are you looking for?" I asked. "A jacket? A sweater?"

I pulled out a dark blue sweatshirt he had been tugging at, but Morris shook his head. "This? This?" I asked, pulling out sweaters. No. No. No. In frustration, Morris yanked a sweatshirt off the hanger and threw it on the bed. But it wasn't what he wanted, either. We finally gave up the search.

I pushed Morris down the hall, while Paul walked beside us, fretting, "Do you want me to push? Is he too heavy?"

A large crowd had already gathered, and the dining room was stiflingly hot. The staff was passing out pointy hats and noisemakers. Paul, Morris, and I wedged ourselves into a row of wheelchairs. Family members, friends, and children of all sizes peppered the white-haired crowd.

The director of the bell ringers was a woman in her eighties named Mabel, who lived outside the nursing home. She informed us that although many of the bell ringers were legally blind, they could still hear quite well. "We're a little nervous," she said, excitedly. "We didn't expect such a crowd!" All the bell ringers were women, except for Ronald from the writing group. The women had gotten their hair done for the occasion and were wearing corsages. Ronald had pinned a red carnation on his green T-shirt.

The group rendered each song very, very slowly to allow Mabel time to move around and shake her finger directly in the face of the designated ringer. For nearly half an hour, they regaled us with "Let me Call you Sweetheart," "My Wild Irish Rose," "In the Good Ole Summer Time," "Put on a Happy Face," and, as the finale, "Jingle Bells."

When the bell ringers were finished, the activities director introduced Suzie Q, a one-woman band who played electric guitar and mandolin. Suzie Q brought the rest of her "band" on tape. She sang Patsy Cline and Elvis songs, old-time hymns, and the "Tennessee Waltz." She got right down to face level, singing to individual members of the crowd and holding their hands. A tiny woman in a white sweater clapped and swayed along with the waltzes.

Then we had the New Year's toast, and a visiting family member initiated a sing-along.

"You could join in," Paul whispered in my ear.

"I don't have a very good voice," I said. "Why don't you sing for both of us?"

Paul snorted at the suggestion, but joined the others in "Silent Night," his soft voice barely audible.

A heavyset woman who looked to be about forty reclined on a rolling bed behind us, making loud gurgling noises. She was swaddled in blankets. Toward the end of the sing-along, a man with an urgent look on his faced tried to weave his way through the wheel-chairs. He finally cut loose and walked jerkily down the hall, a wet spot on the back of his sweatpants.

From time to time, Paul leaned over and whispered something incongruously romantic. "You're the most beautiful woman here." "Have I told you I love you today?"

Once he put his hand on my back, then quickly withdrew it. "I'm sorry. I hope I'm not embarrassing you," he said, then shifted into third person, speaking as if he were an observer in the room. "He only had eyes for her."

As soon as the singing stopped, Paul rose to his feet.

"Shouldn't we ask Morris if he wants to stay for refreshments?" I suggested.

Paul turned reluctantly to Morris, who replied, "Yeah, yeah, ppppppunch."

"Shoot," Paul said and sat down.

It soon became apparent that Morris needed help negotiating his cup and cookies. Unfamiliar with the extent of his disabilities, I hadn't immediately taken on the task of feeding him. But then I looked over and saw his cup teetering precariously toward his lap, his head tilted awkwardly to one side, and a piece of cookie hanging from the side of his mouth. Meanwhile, up front, one of the bell ringers had spilled punch, and a puddle was forming beneath her feet. Someone else tipped his paper plate, causing M&Ms to skitter across the floor.

When we finally returned to Paul's room I collapsed on the bed.

"Are you tired?" Paul asked, easing into his recliner.

"How can I be tired?" I answered wearily. "I haven't done anything. Yet I feel drained of all energy."

"Like you've been driving for hours with the brakes on?"

"Yes. Exactly."

"It's this place. We've got to do something to reanimate our-selves," Paul said.

"I need a jolt of electricity."

"Did you notice that I inched this chair closer to the bed?" Paul asked.

"Yes. How'd you manage that?"

"With an effort of great will. Come over here a minute," Paul said, motioning with his hand. "I was thinking that I have never held you properly in my arms. That's not right."

I stood in front of the chair and allowed Paul to turn my body around and pull me onto his lap.

"I'm afraid I'll crush you," I said, shifting my weight over his bony knees and bracing myself on the bed with one hand.

"You won't," he said confidently. "Now, that's better. We have about half an hour before dinner. What would you like to do?"

I noticed that Paul had made several other small changes in the room. The blinds were closed, and the privacy curtain had been drawn to partially obscure the bed and chair.

We embraced for several minutes, planting little kisses on each other's faces. The kissing got harder and longer. We opened our mouths and bit each other's lips. I ran my hands over Paul's arms and felt his reedy biceps. Paul fondled my breasts, first over my blouse, then under it. "They're bigger that I thought," he murmured. "A perfect mouthful." Paul reached for my hand and pushed it onto the bulge in his pants.

"I'm surprised at my own boldness," Paul said, dizzily. "Let's get out of here."

"It's almost dinner time," I said in a hoarse voice. "What about your meds?"

"You would think they'd have accommodations for something like this," Paul said.

"Like what?" I teased.

"Man and woman stuff. The embrace of the ages."

"I think they do, but you have to be married to use them. I don't think they planned for something—of this sort." We smiled goofily at each other.

"It's good we can laugh about it," Paul said. "It's so hard to find someone, and then when you do, you can't enjoy it. But I'll try." He slipped his hand up my skirt and began stroking my thigh.

I heard voices and peeked around the curtain. An aide was standing in the doorway across the hall, talking to another aide. Nervously, I jumped off Paul's lap. "Let's just sit and talk for a while," I suggested, positioning myself on the edge of the bed.

"My grandmother had an enormous influence on me," Paul said. "Still does. I can just hear her, 'You've gotten as far as you have with her because of what I taught you.'"

"What did she teach you?"

"To be a gentleman. Not so much by words as by inference. To respect a woman. She scared me, really. I was afraid to be anything *but* a gentleman. What kind of wallpaper do you have in your bedroom?"

"Wallpaper? None. I have clouds painted on the walls."

"I always wanted to do that. Did you paint the North Star on the ceiling?"

"No, but that's a good idea."

"When I was a young married man, we had a big old farmhouse out on Grand River. We had two kids, and we didn't want any more. We used to entertain friends—two couples especially who came to play pinochle and canasta. We played a lot of cards in those days. One of our friends, Bill Miller, used to kid me about the wallpaper in our bedroom. It had cabbage roses all over it, which I liked, because I was a gardener. Bill used to say, 'You've got to get rid of that damn wallpaper. Otherwise, you're gonna have half a dozen kids running around here!'" Paul grinned at the memory. "He was a funny guy."

We gazed at each other.

"Here's something that hadn't occurred to me before," Paul said. "It might not work. It's been a long time."

"I have no expectations," I assured him.

"Well, I DO!"

"We'll just have to see what happens," I said, amused at his response. "How long has it been, anyway?"

"Several years. Many years."

"For lack of desire or opportunity?"

"I did feel the desire from time to time, but Lila was sick for three or four years with the cancer, and all those operations . . ."

"Here's another thing," I said. "Birth control. I'm still a woman of childbearing age, you know."

"A woman of childbearing age," Paul repeated, drawing out the phrase. "A childbearer. Childbearers are good. That's how we all got here, fooling around with childbearers."

"Still, I wouldn't want to be one myself."

"Of course not. It would probably scare me to death if that happened, anyway."

We fell silent, mulling over the possibilities.

"You must come to my house," I said.

"Yes. When?"

"We could go tonight after dinner, if you're not too tired."

"I'm a ball of fire. Will there be any irate boyfriends charging in?"

"No, I told you, there's no one. Just you."

"That's what I wanted to hear," Paul said, squeezing my hand.

"We need to wipe these smiles off our faces, or people in the dining room will think something's up," I said.

"Something's up all right, darlin'," Paul said.

"You look like a teenager," I said.

"I FEEL like a teenager!"

WE RUSHED through dinner. The plan was to go to my house and be back by ten, in time for Paul's evening meds. But Dan made a surprise visit and sat down at the table with us, striking up a leisurely conversation as he shuffled through Paul's mail.

"Publisher's Clearinghouse says that you may have already won a million dollars," Dan reported.

Paul rolled his eyes.

"What are you doing tomorrow, Dad?" Dan asked.

"Just sitting by the phone, waiting for you to call, like I always do, day after day." Paul sighed for dramatic effect.

"That's right, lay on the guilt," Dan said. "How'd you like to come over for dinner?"

"That sounds lovely, Dan, but I don't have time to discuss the particulars right now."

"Why, are you two going out?"

Paul and I exchanged looks. "I thought I'd take Paul down to Hart Plaza for some ice-skating under the stars," I said. "You know, one of those romantic New Year's Eve dates like you see in the movies."

"Yes, but she'll probably do all the skating," Paul added. "I'm just going along for the ride. Don't you have to be going now?"

"I guess so," Dan said, looking surprised. "Here's your hat, now where's the door?" He gathered up the mail. "I'll call you in the morning."

"Thank you, Dan," Paul said, rising as if to show him out.

When Dan had rounded the corner of the dining room, Paul said, "I thought he'd never leave! Let's get out of here before anyone else drops by!"

MY HOUSE was a twenty-five-minute drive from the nursing home.

"What are you thinking right now?" Paul asked as we headed eastward.

"I'm reviewing the conversation we just had with Dan. I like him."

"Dan is a good boy. And a good husband and father. When he comes in the door at night, he finishes up whatever dishes are in the sink and runs the vacuum cleaner, as if he and Susan had a pact that she wouldn't have to overdo it. But I think Susan sees me as competition for his attention."

"Have you talked to Dan about that?"

"No, and I'm not going to, either. He and I get along just fine the way things are. The only real difference in opinion we ever had was when we discussed my options after Lila died. Everybody assumed I would go first, so we hadn't made any arrangements. I wanted to hire a woman to come in to cook and clean, but Dan thought I should have full-time nursing care. 'I don't trust you to make this decision,' he said, which cut me to the core. 'You don't think I can assess my own abilities?' I said. 'No, Dad, not at this time, I don't,' he said. As they say in the South, that was one sorry day."

"So that's how you ended up in a nursing home?"

"Well, not right away. First I moved up here and got a little apartment, assisted living, they call it. Dan lived close by and would check on me. Everything was going along fine until one day I was walking Penny by the river, and I lost my balance. The water was only up to my waist, but after that, Dan kept pushing the nursing home. He was afraid I'd fall into the river and drown."

"I'd have worried about the same thing," I said.

"There are worse ways to die. I had to give Penny to Dan and Susan when I moved. But they didn't care about her like I did. Susan spent all her time with the children, and Penny went begging for attention. She was the best-behaved little dog, too. Lila and I used to be gone for twelve, fourteen hours at a time, and Penny never once went in the house. You'd open up the back door, and there she'd be, looking up at you with those big brown eyes. Poor little Penny."

"At least you can see her when you visit Dan."

"No, I can't. They gave her away."

"Oh! That's too bad!"

"You lose more than your independence when you move into a nursing home. You have to start a whole new life. And it doesn't come with all the fringe benefits of your previous life."

I nodded in the dark.

"But this fringe benefit is a surprise and a blessing," Paul said, placing his hand on my knee. "More than I ever could have hoped for."

As WE walked up the back steps into my kitchen, Paul said, "This entrance reminds me of a house I was in about sixty-five years ago. On New Year's Eve, too. Remind me to tell you that story later."

I gave him a tour of my small house, ending with the bedroom. Paul said, "I like the clouds." I had bought pink satin sheets for this occasion, smiling secretly as I waited in the checkout line at Bed, Bath, and Beyond. I had read in a book called *Caring for the Parkinson's Patient* that satin sheets helped a person slide out of bed. I knew that in South Carolina, Paul had tied a thick silk cord to the bedpost in order to pull himself upright. But I figured he wouldn't have the upper-body strength for that now.

We began kissing and fumbling around in the dark. Once undressed, we slipped between the sheets, which were shockingly cold, and continued kissing and fondling. After about half an hour, Paul said, "I'm sorry, honey. I guess the prostate cancer affected me more than I thought. What can I do for you?"[1]

"Tell me the story of the back steps," I said, resting my head on his shoulder.

"I was in my late teens at the time," Paul began. "It was New Year's Eve, and we were all going to a party at Mary Ellen Riley's house. A big mansion in Rosedale Park, or at least it seemed so to me. Mary Ellen was a high-society girl. There were four of us going together: my friend Andrew Lumley, whose date was Rosemary Anderson, me, and my date, June Phillips. I dated Rosemary from time to time, too, but not that night. Rosemary was faster than June. We'd lie on the couch and kiss—no hanky-panky, just kissing—and she'd say, 'You can go a littler farther' and take my hand and place it on her breast. June, on the other hand, was a very proper girl, although she and Rosemary were good friends. June's family had a lot of money. She had maids and tutors and went to finishing school, where she learned how to talk, greet people, and take a gentleman's hat. She used to practice walking around the house with a book on her head. Her parents were very proper people.

"So we went to this party at Mary Ellen's, and it broke up around one o'clock. I walked June home, which was four or five blocks from the Riley house. June's parents had gone to a party and were still out. The house was dark. We sat in two straight-back chairs, talking and holding hands. I don't know why we sat in those chairs. We could have sat somewhere more comfortable, because we weren't doing anything, but June had a sense of propriety about her. Then we saw the headlights of her father's car sweep through the living room. June went crazy. 'Oh, they're home! They'll never understand! My father will never believe us if we tell him we're innocent!' I tried to calm her down, but she was getting hysterical.

"When we heard the key in the front door, I ran like a shot through the kitchen, down four or five stairs to the landing where the back door was. I pulled on the door, but it wouldn't open. I struggled to find the lock, but it was dark, and I couldn't get it undone. By then, June's parents were coming through the front door. I could hear June trying to talk them into going right to bed. She was saying she knew how tired they must be, and she'd make her mother some hot chocolate and bring it up to her. Her mother said, 'What's the matter with you, June? I don't want any hot chocolate!'

"Since I couldn't get out the door, I turned to my right, where the basement steps were, and snuck down the steps as quietly as I could. I felt my way around the basement, looking up at the windows. Upstairs, I could hear June still trying to talk her mother into some hot chocolate. My plan was to find something to stand on and crawl out one of the basement windows. I could see the lights of the paint store on the corner of Grand River.

"But then I knocked over a water bucket. It skated across the floor and slammed into the furnace—one of those tin furnaces with the huge arms reaching out from all directions. I ran up the stairs and through the kitchen, where June and her parents were standing. All three of them had these astonished looks on their faces. Her father had a wet stogy hanging halfway out of his mouth. As I was backing my way out of the house, I said in one big rush, 'June and I weren't doing anything at all just sitting and talking in straight chairs and then we saw the car lights and June got panicky and sent me out the back way but I couldn't get out because the door was locked so I tried to get out a basement window and knocked over a water bucket and that's the truth Mr. Phillips I swear it and I have nothing but the utmost respect for June and thanks for a nice evening June.' And I ran out into the night.

"It was one of those unseasonably mild winter evenings, just like tonight. But still, it was raining, and I had to walk two or three miles home to Redford. I got chilled on my way home and stopped at Hinkley's Bakery, which was about halfway. Mr. Hinkley was there, baking for the next day, and he let me in to get warm. He said, 'You go over and sit next to the stove, and I'll bring you a cup of coffee.' When I was warmed up, I walked the rest of the way home.

"My grandmother was asleep, of course, but I went right in and sat on the edge of her bed and told her the whole story. She was laughing all the way through it; I could feel the bed shaking.

"The next morning, about nine o'clock, the phone rang. My grandmother called out, 'It's for you, a Mrs. Phillips!' I hollered back, 'Tell them I died!' She said, 'Shush, she can hear you!' So I went to the phone. Mrs. Phillips said, 'We are all very upset, and Mr. Phillips will never believe your story. But I believe you and June, and if you want to see June again, you'll have to come on a Thursday night. That's Mr. Phillips's lodge night, and he's always out.'

"After that, June's friends treated me like I was some kind of royalty, coming up with a good story like that on the spur of the moment. But of course, I had just reported the facts. I've always believed there's no story better than a true story."

An hour or so later, after we had napped some, I stood by the side of the bed, tugging on Paul's arms to help him up. "Wait," he said, rolling over stiffly. "I have to get a leg over the side to get a foothold." When he got his leg into place, I pushed him into a sitting position. He rested on the edge of the bed, weak and dizzy. Oh no, I thought, he's too tired to move. But then he forced himself off the bed and stumbled into the bathroom, knocking over the cat bowls on his way through the kitchen. When he returned to the bedroom, he stood limply while I inserted his arms into his shirtsleeves.

"I dribbled a few drops on my underpants when I was taking them off," Paul said sheepishly. "Several drops."

"Do you want to put them back on?" I asked.

"No, I want to throw them away," he said. "I'm so sorry." Paul slumped against me as I buttoned his shirt, zipped his pants, buckled his belt, and tied his shoes. "It's a shame you have to go out this time of night," he said. "I feel bad about that, too."

On the drive back to what Paul kept referring to as the "dorm," he gently laid his hand on my thigh. "What are you thinking?"

"I'm worried that I kept you out too late, and you've gotten overly tired."

"When you're tired, you're just tired. It doesn't mean you're going to die."

"Right. OK."

"When you get back home, call me and say, 'Good night, I love you.' Will you do that?"

"Yes."

As we drove through the night, Paul added more details to the phone message: "Call me and say, 'The car is right side up. I'm in the house, the door is locked, I'm eating my cereal, good night, I love you.' I like your house," Paul added. "I'd like to take you to South Carolina with me some time. It's a beautiful place."

"I'd like that," I said. "I've never spent much time in the South, but I am going to Phoenix in March."

"What for?"

"To give a paper at a conference."

"Do you like your job?"

"I love it. I can't think of anything more wonderful than being a professor. You get to read, write, explore new ideas. Your time is mostly your own. The pay's not great, but that doesn't matter so much."

"That's good," Paul nodded.

"What's the story about where we went tonight?" I asked.

"I'll tell them you took me to some friends' house—academics— and I couldn't get a word in edgewise. I had to deliver a paper to get their attention."

5 A LAMENTABLE SITUATION

Paul was frail. His heart was weak; he had trouble controlling his bladder; his vision in one eye was poor and he wore a patch over the other eye; he had a bad knee and poor circulation in his legs. The most serious condition, however, was Parkinson's disease, a neurological disorder characterized by tremor, slow and reduced body movements, and muscle rigidity.

I read a lot about Parkinson's when I was first getting to know Paul. In 1997, more than half a million people in America had Parkinson's disease, named after James Parkinson, the British physician who first described the symptoms in 1817. Famous people who suffered from Parkinson's at the time included Muhammad Ali, former world heavyweight boxing champion; Pope John Paul II; and the actor Michael J. Fox. Now, in 2007, approximately 3 percent of the American population over sixty-five is affected by Parkinson's, with men nearly twice as likely as women to get the disease.[1] Parkinson's involves the destruction of neurons that are critical to coordination, as well as the depletion of dopamine, a chemical necessary for certain structures in the brain to communicate with each other. Symptoms of Parkinson's, besides palsy, include bradykinesia (slow or reduced movement), poor balance, disturbed gait (shuffling), sudden immobility ("frozen feet"), stooped posture, blank facial expression (the Parkinson's mask), reduced volume of speech or aphasia (inability to speak) in later stages, memory impairment, muscle atrophy, sexual dysfunction, incontinence, and weight loss. Paul experienced all these symptoms in different degrees. When I met him, he weighed around 150, having lost more than 40 pounds. He had had Parkinson's for twenty years.

Parkinson's varies in severity and usually progresses slowly. A common clinical scale identifies five stages: in stage 1, only one side of the body is affected; in stage 2, both sides are affected, but balance is not impaired; in stage 3, balance is affected; in stage 4, the person is functionally disabled, and in stage 5, the patient is confined to a bed or wheelchair.[2] With medication, Paul could function at stage 2 or 3 for several hours a day, and assume most of the ADLs (activities of daily living) by which nursing homes assess the level of care needed by residents: he bathed and dressed himself (except for buttoning, shoe tying, and putting on socks); fed himself; used the toilet on his own; walked independently with a cane or motored around in a scooter; and was able to communicate his needs clearly.

Paul relied on a common treatment for Parkinson's, a drug called levodopa. Combined with another drug called carbidopa, it is sold under the brand name Sinemet. Levodopa does not cure or even slow the advance of Parkinson's, but it can drastically increase a person's ability to function. It allowed Paul to maintain a reasonable amount of independence and control over his daily life. Timing of the doses was critical, however; when the nursing home staff was late with his pills, or too much time had lapsed between doses, Paul would have tremors. Other conditions, like stress and fatigue, affected how well (and for how long) he responded to medication. Sometimes Paul experienced the "on-off" phenomenon, with periods of normal functioning interspersed with short episodes of trembling and immobility.

Yet Paul did not think of himself as disabled and never used the word "disease" when referring to Parkinson's. He talked about his "condition," a word that to him suggested less disability and more possibility. Most of the time, Paul focused on the positive aspects of his life. "Not many people who have had Parkinson's for over twenty years can get around and make themselves heard," he often said. "I feel very fortunate."

In fact, Morris, who also had Parkinson's, was a daily reminder of how bad things could get. Once a fast-talking public relations man, Morris could now barely make himself heard, much less understood, even on good days. He had been quite handsome, well over six feet tall, with broad shoulders and steel gray hair. Now he was caved in upon himself, so weak that he had to be strapped into a wheelchair. His hands were rigid, and his fingers appeared to be welded together. He wore a diaper. And recently he had been showing signs of dementia. Morris spent all day, every day, in a wheelchair until the aides put him to bed at 7:00 p.m., where he stayed until they got him up at 6:00 a.m.

Parkinson's meant Morris did everything very slowly and ineptly. The aides would feed Morris last and rush him through a meal. Paul was often distressed over the conduct of both Morris and the aides at meal times.

"Why don't they let Morris feed himself?" I asked Paul one day.

"He spills it all over his clothes. But my position is, so what? Who cares if he makes a mess? Why not allow a man the simple dignity of holding his own fork?"

Paul was constantly intervening between Morris and the aides: "Look, he needs more time; slow down." "Morris, don't be so contrary; they're just trying to do their job."

Morris would get mad and refuse to take his pills. The aides would sneak up on him when he was breathing through his mouth and drop in the pills. This would make Morris furious, but all he could do was make his mouth a hard line and stare at the ceiling. "It really takes the polish off things," Paul said.

Morris's wife, Bea, came regularly to supervise his care. She was an attractive woman in her mid-seventies, although the right side of her face was pulled downward, giving her a slightly lopsided look. Paul referred to Bea as "the hostess" because of the way she scurried around the dining room serving coffee and ice cream to the other residents. Also, he couldn't remember her name.

"The hostess was here today," he would report over the phone. "It was 'do this', and 'don't do that,' and 'now look what a mess you've made of things!' She means well, but she sometimes makes things worse. She talks about Morris like he's not here. Well, to be fair, sometimes he isn't, but then again, sometimes he is, and she doesn't acknowledge it. She'll say to me, in this conspiratorial tone, 'Boy, he's really out of it today.'"

Bea would talk to me, too, about both Morris and Paul, as we all sat around the table at lunchtime. "I believe Morris has gotten worse," she said one day. "See how he looks around like that? He's not here when he does that." Morris was scanning the ceiling with his bug eyes.

"Sometimes he just sits with his mouth open, letting the drool slide down his face," Bea said. "He's confused, too. The other day he said, 'Bring me my typewriter.' He used to be a writer, you know. And I said, 'Your typewriter's not here, honey.' He kept insisting that it was. I said, 'Well, then, where is it?' He said, 'I don't know, but it's here somewhere.' When he argues like that I just try to ignore it and walk away."

"It must be hard to adjust to the changes in him," I said. "I guess you can never fully prepare for something like that."

"When he was diagnosed, I read all the literature. I knew what to expect at the end. I just hope God takes him before he becomes a total vegetable. Paul seems to be holding up pretty well, though."

"Paul, we're talking about you," I said, smiling at him.

"Were your ears burning?" Bea asked.

"They were beginning to curl a bit at the edges," Paul said.

"When did you first get Parkinson's? Bea asked.

"I've had it for years," Paul said. "I had it long before I knew I had it."

"Morris was forty-nine," Bea offered. "He had to retire at fifty-eight. It's been a long haul."

"I was sitting in a doctor friend's office in South Carolina," Paul said. "He asked me why my hand was shaking. I said, 'Oh, I built a greenhouse this week, and I guess I overdid it a little bit.' I assumed I had overtaxed my muscles."

"So you thought," Bea said.

"That little shaking in my right hand had happened many times before, but I didn't think much of it. My friend said, 'I want you to go see someone about that,' and he gave me the name of a specialist."

"Morris has been pretty healthy except for the Parkinson's," Bea said. "He did have a hip replacement—well, so did I—and it hasn't given him a bit of trouble since. The doctor said, 'He'll walk again.' I said, 'With the help of you and what miracle?' But he did walk. He used a walker, but he was up and moving. He did better than I did with that hip replacement. But then I got a brain tumor. They took out all kinds of things, including my right ear. I don't have control over the right side of my face now. I can't wink my right eye. It took me a long time to recover. But I didn't take long enough, really, because I went right back to taking care of him as soon as I could. He just kept getting worse, and it wore us both out." She looked at Morris wearily.

"Is there any chocolate ice cream?" Paul asked.

"Let me check," Bea offered, rising from her chair.

Morris looked at me and said something I didn't understand.

"Sherry? Who's Sherry?" I asked.

"Ch-ch-ch-ch-erry?"

"No, dear, there's no cherry ice cream," Bea interpreted.

"B-b-b-b-b-but . . ."

"There is no cherry, Morris. She was mistaken. She's human! Everyone makes mistakes!"

"There, now, you've caused a family feud," Paul said mildly.

Constantine, from the writing group, was sitting with us then, and he gave Morris a pained look.

Over a period of months, various other men had come and gone from this conversational circle, which the aides called "the men's table," because every other table was occupied exclusively by women. Constantine sat with us for a few weeks until he was hospitalized. When he returned, he was placed on another floor. (They don't hold your room long in a nursing home.) Constantine had been in the merchant marines and liked to talk about that. Morris was sociable, too, when he was feeling up to it, and he would occasionally make a concerted effort to start a conversation. He would stammer something undecipherable, and Paul and I would try to figure it out.

"A little slower, Morris," I'd say.

"Take one word at a time," Paul added, demonstrating by hopping his fingers across the table as if jumping an opponent's checkers.

"Tttttttttthere are ffffffffourteen ppppppeople here."

"Let me check your arithmetic," I said, looking around the room. "Yup. Fourteen, all right."

"Hhhhyyyyyyyyougggggggoooootttaptomototon."

"Did you get that?" Paul asked me.

"No," I said.

"Take it slower, buddy," Paul said, encouragingly.

"I—hhhear—you—ggggot—a—ppro—motion," Morris said.

"Oh, Paul, did you tell him that?"

"Do—you—gggget—more—mmmmoney?" Morris asked.

"A little bit," I said, "but mostly a shift in responsibilities and workload. It's just what I wanted."

"Ahhhh, gggoood," Morris said.

"Are you two going out tonight?" Constantine asked.

"No," said Paul. "I don't have any money."

"Let her pay," Constantine said.

"There you go, Paul. I've been saying that all along," I said, nudging his arm.

"Yes, she's tried," Paul agreed. "But a man has his pride."

"There's no moon out tonight, but it could still be romantic," Constantine said. "I'm an old man. I can only dream of such things." Constantine had just lost his wife of sixty years.

"That reminds me of a poem by William Butler Yeats," I said, "which he wrote around the age of seventy: 'I pray—for fashion's word is out / and prayer comes round again— / That I may seem, though I die old, / a foolish, passionate man.'"

"So true, so true my love," Paul said, taking my hand.

"Mmmy bbbirthday's nnneext week," Morris offered.

"Your birthday's next week?" I repeated.

"Wwweeek fffrom tttoday."

"How old will you be?"

Morris stopped to think. Sssseventy-tttwo."

"Great," I said. "Although Paul's got you beat by ten years."

Morris started singing a Frank Sinatra tune.

"Bbye, bye bbaby . . ."

Paul recognized the song immediately and hummed along. "Bye bye baby, remember you're my baby, when others give you the eye . . ." Morris enunciated every word perfectly.

"God, that's an oldie," Paul smiled.

"Hey, you can sing!" I said.

"I—used—ttto—sing—very—wwell," Morris replied, his eyes bright.

Later, when Paul and I were leaving the table, Morris pulled on Paul's sleeve and mumbled, "It—mmust—be—electrifffying."

"How's that?" Paul asked.

"I—wwwwish—" Morris continued.

Paul repeated the words: "I wish . . ."

"You—cccould—ffigure—out—"

"I could figure out . . ."

"A—wway—for—mme—to—rride—on—your—cccoattails."

PAUL WAS a companionable man, but he found mealtimes stressful. It wasn't just the tensions surrounding Morris and the aides. Paul's own condition made eating an ordeal. It was especially hard for him to cut, scoop, and spear. He would chase a pea around his plate for two or three minutes. After struggling to peel the plastic film off a single-serving container of coffee creamer, he'd give up and stab it with a fork. When Paul ate with his hands (much easier to control than a knife and fork), he would drop food on his clothes and litter the floor. He finally agreed to wear a bib, but this compromised his sense of gentlemanly propriety. Eating required perseverance. As time went on, Paul just lost the energy for it.

Plus the food usually wasn't worth the bother, which was too bad, because Paul had always been a man of appetite. He once told me a story about a time in his middle forties when he was a traveling salesman on the road. He had stopped for lunch at a back roads diner. He was hungry and found the food so delicious that when he got back in the car, he couldn't stop thinking about it. So he stopped at a second diner down the road and ate *another* lunch. Paul enjoyed telling stories about food. One time when his kids were teenagers, he and Iris went to a New Year's Eve party. Paul had been a social drinker, and he didn't want to get drunk over the course of a long evening. So he ordered a dinner that he thought would absorb the alcohol. He told the waiter exactly how the kitchen was to prepare it: "I want a plate of hard-boiled eggs," he said. "Slice them lengthwise and arrange them in overlapping circles around the plate. Salt and pepper them lightly, and drizzle them with olive oil. Put some black olives in the middle. If you have any, lay some bay leaves around the edge of the plate. The whole arrangement should resemble a sunflower." When Paul's dinner came, exactly as requested, it was the joke of the evening.

These days, food came in heavy, wet mounds. A dinner tray might be laden with creamed chicken, dumplings, potatoes and gravy, steamed broccoli, white cake with white frosting, chocolate ice cream, and a single slice of wheat bread wrapped in cellophane, plus coffee, milk, grape juice, and the cup of "pro-pudding" the dieticians insisted on adding to fatten Paul up, although he never ate it. I'd look at the heaving tray and start removing things, trying to make it look more appealing.

"I don't suppose you'll eat this bread," I'd say, putting it to the side.

"I like bread and butter, I really do," Paul said. "But I can never get to it. There's always so much other food to attend to."

"Yes, I can see how things pile up."

"Same thing with peanut butter and jelly. I love it, but I never get to eat it. My jar of beautiful raspberry jam is growing grass on the windowsill. A peanut butter and jelly sandwich needs to be enjoyed on its own, with a glass of cold milk. It is a thing unto itself. There's no place for it here. The food trays come fast and full, three times a day. There's no opportunity to enjoy the simple pleasure of a single sandwich, eaten when you're slightly hungry but not so hungry that you wolf it down."

Paul sometimes lost track of time, which also affected his appetite. Sleep disturbance is another common consequence of Parkinson's, and living in a nursing home exacerbates the problem. Paul often slept in his recliner—with the door wide open because the staff preferred it that way. But then he'd hear all the noise in the hall and be awakened by the "door slammers"—aides and nurses moving in and out of rooms all night long. He joked that the door slammers should get together with the bell ringers and put on a concert, which should be pretty good, because the door slammers practiced every night. Amid all the commotion, Paul slept in fits and starts. He would awaken at four and wonder was it morning or afternoon. The disorientation made him feel like an inmate.

One day Paul telephoned with an announcement. "I've made a decision. I'm going to sleep through the night and get up in the morning refreshed, alert, and energized. None of this sleeping off and on all day and night."

"That sounds like an excellent idea," I said approvingly. "You do sleep a lot."

"I know, and it bothers me. I just can't seem to get caught up."

"Maybe you're bored. Could you find something to occupy your time?"

"Like what? I can't chase nurses."

"Well, I suppose you COULD chase nurses, but I was thinking more along the lines of reading the great books or writing your memoirs."

"You wouldn't care if I chased nurses?" Paul said in a wounded tone.

"I can't tell you what to do."

"Yes, you can," he said, seriously. "You certainly can."

"Let's put it this way. I would prefer that you NOT chase nurses."

"Like I said, then," Paul said, cheerily, "I can't chase nurses."

Paul did try to get himself on a regular schedule, but the effort didn't last long. He had to get up two or three times a night to go to the bathroom, which took a while, given his limited range of motion, and then he was wide awake and couldn't get back to sleep. Then he was tired the next day, so he'd take a nap. Pretty soon he was right back to his old patterns, sleeping off and on all day and night.

This made it very difficult to arrange a date.

One morning when we were talking on the phone, we made plans to have breakfast together at Bedford the next morning before I went to work. Later that afternoon, Paul called to say that my tray had just arrived.

"What do you mean?" I said, confused. "I thought I was coming tomorrow."

"I was sleeping when the aide came to get me for dinner," Paul explained. "I told her, 'Before I forget, I'd like to order a tray for my friend, who's coming to eat with me.' I thought it was morning already. So there's a whole tray of food waiting here for you."

It seemed to me that we lived in completely different time zones.

"It's been days since you were here," Paul would complain over the phone.

"I left exactly two and a half hours ago," I'd say, deeply absorbed in some project.

"Time here, I measure it in weeks and months. It's endless."

Or I'd call him from work around midmorning and find him sleeping.

"Why aren't you up yet?" I'd ask, slightly irritated.

"I was sleepy. It was another long night, up and down. I was up at quarter to six, and I wanted so much to call you. I struggled with that and then talked myself out of it."

"Oh, Paul," I'd say, softening. "You don't have to fight those urges all the time. Go ahead and call."

"Thank you, darlin'. You are quite a package."

"Thank you. And so are you."

"What have you been thinking about?" he'd ask.

"Oh, all kinds of things. I don't know where to start. What have you been thinking about?"

"How I'm not being fair to you. How the circumstances are so unfortunate. I've been tallying up the pluses and minuses. So far there are a lot of pluses. If I had a longer future, I'd ask you to marry me. But up on Prospect Hill, things don't look so good."

"I don't need to be married, Paul."

"Marriage is an indication of love," Paul said. "Or crazy-fool rashness."

"In our case, it would be both," I said, swallowing the lump in my throat.

"Yesterday, when you couldn't be here, I was swinging on a manure spreader, and the air was getting fouled up."

Paul's homespun metaphors always made me laugh. "What were you doing on a manure spreader?"

"An aide—that skinny, young one—asked me, 'Is she still your girl?' in a smirky tone. I thought about calling you, but I didn't want to interrupt your work. I was among my dreads, and that yellow pad you left here was beckoning, saying, 'Come on!' So I wrote you a little poem. But I don't want to read it over the phone. I feel silly."

"Paul! Just knowing that you wrote me a poem makes me very happy."

"You'll have to come over to hear it. Meanwhile, I'll sing you this, in my best Ray Charles voice:

I love you so much it hurts me.
Darlin' that's why I'm so blue.
I'm so afraid to go to bed at night,
Afraid of losing you.
I love you so much it hurts me.
And there's nothing I can do.
I want to hold you, my dear,
Forever and ever
I love you so much it hurts me."

6 THOSE LITTLE
ORDINARY THINGS

Paul and I were making a shopping list.

"Those toaster things, breakfast food, what do you call them?" Paul asked. "But not blueberry flavored. Blueberries have practically no taste. I like blackberry, but that's probably too exotic. Let's say strawberry or raspberry."

"Anything else?" I said.

"And some eye drops," Paul added. "I've got an irritation, a little cold maybe, in my good eye. I've had it for three days. I asked the nurse for eye drops, but all they had was artificial tears. It really bothers me, because it's the only eye I've got. I'd just as soon lose my leg as my eye."

"By the way, what happened to your left eye?" I asked. Paul wore a black patch over the empty socket.

"I was a kid, playing in the yard, climbing a tree with my friend. It was a—what's the name of that tree with the banana pods on it?"

"Catalpa?"

Paul grinned. "You're really something. Only about nineteen out of a hundred people would know that! Anyway, there was a rusty nail sticking out of that tree, and I came up against it."

"Ouch. And the rest is history."

"Isn't that something?" Paul said. "In that one little minute, my life changed forever. Some people treat you differently when you wear a patch on your eye. But I think it worked to my advantage as a salesman. That is, after I got people over the idea that they were dealing with a pirate."

Paul had already told me, in his modest, amused way, that at one time in his life, he could sell just about anything to anybody. Once, for the pleasure and the practice, he had talked someone into buying a dirty ashtray.

"Why don't you take a little nap and rest your eye?" I said. "I'll go shopping."

"Wait! You can't go now. I don't have any money for you yet."

"That's OK. I'm not worried. You could give me an IOU."

"No, it's the principle of the thing," Paul insisted. "I don't want to make an errand girl out of you, or a cheapskate out of me."

"I don't mind, really Paul."

"It's not right," Paul said. "It's been so long since I had my hand in my back pocket, I've forgotten how to get there. I want to *do* for you, but here I am, spread-eagled."

"I don't see you that way, but I know what you mean. "

"To his credit, Dan is very good about money. He'll say, 'How much cash does my boy need now?' and roll his eyes in that funny way of his. I'm proud of the way he handles things."

Although Paul and Dan were close, they didn't spend a lot of time together. In his early fifties, Dan was building a business and raising two kids.

"As soon as he puts one foot through the door, the other one's halfway out," Paul said of Dan's visits.

Just a quick telephone call from Dan would have met Paul's need for reassurance. When it didn't come, he worried.

One day, Paul was feeling a little off.

"What's wrong?" I asked.

"I haven't heard from Dan for some time," Paul said.

"When was the last time you talked?"

"He was here to fix my chair. The arm was wobbly. But that was over a week ago, and he hasn't called since. He usually calls to tell me he's all right. They'd call me if he was sick or in an accident, wouldn't they?"

"Surely," I said. "Does Dan know that you worry when he doesn't call?"

"Yes, I've made that perfectly clear. It doesn't take much to pick up a phone and say, 'I'm fine,' especially with phones everywhere these days, even in the car."

I didn't know how to respond. I understood Paul's feelings, but I didn't call my mother very often, either.

"For a while, he called morning and night when he was on the road, just to tell me where he was going and that he had gotten there OK."

"Does his wife call you when Dan doesn't?"

"She did at first," Paul said. "Right after I moved here. But not much anymore."

"Why don't you call them?" I asked.

"I do once in a while, but I don't want to be a bother or a burden."

"If you're really worried, though, this seems like the time to call."

"Will you dial for me? I need some water."

While Paul fortified himself with a drink, I dialed the number.

"It's ringing," I said, handing him the receiver.

Paul got the answering machine and left a message: "Susan, it's Paul. Call us, won't you? I've been worried. Just want to know that everything's OK. I'd like you to call me back when you get in. Thanks."

Paul's speech was soft, low and shaky. He didn't seem much relieved after he hung up.

"What shall we do now?" he asked, trying to pull himself out of the gloom.

"I brought my computer," I said. "In case you feel like working on your life story."

"I don't think I could concentrate. I'm preoccupied with Dan. When things aren't going well, when I'm worried about something, I don't like this place very much. But then, nobody said I had to like it, did they?"

Paul started shuffling through some papers on the dresser. He pulled out a picture of his church in South Carolina, which a friend had sent in a Christmas card.

"Just look at the finish on that," Paul mused. "Beautiful. I went down the aisle in that church. I could just hear some of them saying, 'Damn Yankee, coming down here and stealing one of our best widows.'"

"You were happy in South Carolina?"

"Loved it. I was head groundskeeper for the university. Perfect job for an outdoorsman. I was healthy as a cowboy in those days." He handed me a card he had just received from the principal of the school where Lila had taught. "Read that," Paul said.

"I'm thinking of our Lila. You made her so happy."

"It was nice of her to say that, don't you think?" Paul said. "Some people take the time to express their feelings. She and Lila were great friends. Now, where is that—" Paul continued to rifle through the cards and papers. "There is a doctor in South Carolina, a wonderful man, who is thoughtful like that. Kind, broad thinker, never judges people. There it is! Right in front of me."

Paul handed me a handwritten note. It began, *"Dear Lila and Paul."*

"Sometimes he addressed it 'Paul and Lila' and sometimes 'Lila and Paul,'" Paul said. "He paid attention to details like that."

"I've been thinking of you two and your struggles. I so wish that I had the ability to help you. I am encouraged, though, by your positive attitudes about your illness. God bless you both."

"I thought it was pretty significant to get a letter like that," Paul said.

"That is one unusual doctor," I agreed.

"I haven't met any half that good since I moved to Michigan."

"What was your wife's illness?" I asked.

"Cancer. Breast cancer. And heart disease."

On his dresser, Paul had several pictures of Lila, along with her driver's license.

"We're just getting to know each other, aren't we?" Paul said.

"Yes. There is quite a bit of distance between us. Have you ever thought about talking to the social worker?"

"That woman with the burr in her voice? I had no idea she was available for conversation. She always seems to be rushing off somewhere."

"I believe the job description of a social worker is 'Good Listener.' She does have a little accent, doesn't she?"

"A burr," Paul said softly.

I smiled at the way he said it.

"You think you know what I mean, don't you?" Paul said.

"Yes, I do."

"I think you do, too," Paul said.

"Did you know that spinach is hermaphroditic?" I asked Paul. He was sitting across from me in a restaurant, gnawing on a spare rib.

"What?" Paul asked.

"Spinach. It's sexually labile," I said, affecting a learned tone.

"What brought that up?" Paul asked, amused.

"I'm on the university's sabbatical leaves committee. I learned that fact today from reading a biologist's research proposal."

"Huh! What's he doing with spinach?"

"He's studying sex-switching plants to better understand the environmental context of their adaptability. This research has the potential to increase crop productivity."

"Isn't that something?" Paul said. "That's an interesting way to spend your time."

"Speaking of spinach," I said, "What'd you have for lunch today?"

"Let me think on that for a moment," he said. Paul was now sawing on a rib with a table knife, trying to extract a bite-size piece. He insisted on ordering challenging pieces of meat, mostly for the smell and the look of them, as well as the memories they invoked.

"There were several different things. By the time I got done separating what I liked from what I didn't, it came down to one or two. There was a slab of Jell-o, orange Jell-o, with nothing in it. No fruit of any kind. You'd think they could have sliced up a banana or something. The Jell-o had been made in a shallow dish, so it was thin. Just a skinny, wobbly square of Jell-o. When I got done jiggling it, I set it aside. There was a bowl of chili, with finely ground meat. Hardly any texture at all, but the taste was all right. And a tuna sandwich. Tuna smashed between two slices of white bread. No attempt at presentation, not even a crisp piece of lettuce to go along with it. Boring, all of it. Boring as hell. You know, the institutional sentence isn't bad, it's just that it lacks *punctuation*."

By now, Paul had amassed a huge pile of sticky napkins. A waitress walked by and leaned down to pick up a fork at the foot of his chair.

"He dropped his fork," she said to me and scurried away.

"Did you notice she spoke of you in the third person?" I said.

"Yes," Paul said. "It's probably my patch. You know, a man wearing a patch over his eye can't see *or* hear properly."

89

"Yes, and an *old* man wearing a patch must be feeble in mind *and* body," I added.

"We'll prove her wrong later in the privacy of my room." Paul whispered. "But first, I must address this piece of pumpkin pie."

BECAUSE OF the Parkinson's, I became acquainted early with Paul's body and its various needs. When I visited, he would usually be in some stage of undress, waiting for an aide to help finish the job.

One afternoon, early in our relationship, I entered Paul's room to find him sitting on the edge of the recliner with his pants legs rolled up to his knees. He was wearing long, white stockings, pulled up as far as his pants legs.

"The aide was here, helping me put these stockings on. They're for my circulation. But she left when she got this far," he explained. "I haven't seen her since, and now they're beginning to cut *off* my circulation."

I knelt down to survey the situation.

"I'll probably have to pull them up from the top, but I have to pull my pants down to do it. Want to help? It's wild territory."

I smiled and probably blushed. "How about if I take a walk down the hall and come back in a few minutes?" I suggested.

"OK."

When I returned, Paul said, "There's a privacy curtain here that I could have pulled. I never noticed it before now. You wouldn't have had to leave."

After we got to know each other better, I would help with Paul's grooming. In a nursing home, residents don't usually get things done for them right away. So they go around with their backs itching terribly in a spot they can't reach or their hair and fingernails needing a trim. In Paul's case, the hair in his ears grew out of control. When I performed this little grooming task, Paul was enormously grateful.

"I won't ask you to do my nose hairs," he said. "That seems a bit much to ask."

"Doesn't your barber do that?"

"Not the one around here. All he does is a basic haircut."

I drew the line in some areas, though. Late one summer afternoon I picked up Paul to take him to my house for dinner. I'd made all the things he liked that I didn't eat in those days—pot roast and banana cream pie made from scratch with whole milk and butter. As soon as we got in the car he said, "Do you know what a Fleet Enema is?"

"Yes," I said, cautiously.

"Can we stop at the drugstore to get one?"

"I suppose so, if that's how you want to spend the evening," I said dryly.

"They cost about a dollar a piece," Paul said, efficiently. "I'll pay you back."

"You're not expecting *me* to give you one, are you?" I asked, a little alarmed. "Because there are some things that I just—"

"No, I can take care of that part myself," Paul said, smiling.

I stopped at a drugstore to purchase the requested item, which came two to a package. Paul waited in the car and seemed immensely pleased when I returned with the bag.

When we got to my house, he said, "Now, how long until dinner?"

"Not long enough for what *you* have in mind," I said.

Paul waited until after we'd eaten and then disappeared as I was reading the newspaper. Some time later, he joined me in the living room.

"I did it!" he said. "I knew I could take care of that problem with a little privacy and the right materials. Plus, you have a nice, cushy rug."

I looked at him warily.

"I didn't make a mess. I just used a few of your Kleenex."

I smiled and shook my head.

"We work well together, don't we?" he said, entwining his fingers in mine. "Don't worry. I washed my hands good, too."

One of the cats jumped up and walked across the back of the couch. The other one sat at our feet, staring at us.

"They're trying to advance the idea of a happy family," Paul said.

WE HAD made arrangements for me to visit Paul after work one Friday night. I was very tired and called to see if Paul was feeling up to it. He was in the middle of changing his pants and talked to me with one leg in, one leg out. He had spilled food on the other pair.

"Did you remember that we had a date tonight?" I asked.

"Oh, yes," Paul said. "I told everyone at the dinner table that my honey was coming."

"What did they say?"

"Nothing. They're used to it."

When I arrived an hour later, I was surprised to find Paul in a state of dishevelment. He looked as though he hadn't shaved in two days, and his hair was matted in the back. He was wearing a bathrobe over his flannel shirt and no pants. The robe was secured with a leather dress belt.

"Are you growing a beard?" I asked delicately.

"My electric razor's not functioning," Paul explained. "The copper screen came off."

"Don't they have someone around here who can give you a wet shave?" I asked.

"Yes, one of the girls said today, 'You can't go to the table like that. Why don't you let me give you a shave?' And I said, 'Well, if I don't get my razor fixed, I'll let you do it tomorrow.' I'd rather shave myself, when I have the proper equipment."

Paul showed me the shaver and the little copper screen, which had a chip out of it, and together we spent at least an hour trying to get the screen back on. While we worked on it, Paul explained what had been going on.

"We had some excitement just before you arrived," he said. "A fire alarm went off. I was looking out into the hallway for you, and that nurse with the loud voice was trying to get me to go back in my room and close the door. I said, 'My girl's coming, and she'll be looking for me to greet her.' And she said, 'There's no one riding the elevator during a fire alarm!' She was adamant, and so was I. I said, half seriously, 'I'm going to have to lodge a complaint if I can't get to my girl. I'll have to notify the authorities.' It was quite a commotion. The alarm was loud enough to hear all the way to 8 Mile Road."

"I guess it was a false alarm, huh?"

"Yes, because there certainly was no fire. But that's why I didn't have my pants on."

"What's with the leather belt?"

"This bathrobe gapes open, even when it's tied. I'm trying to maintain some dignity. Promise you won't peek?"

"Do you have any underpants on?" I asked suspiciously. I knew that Paul often skipped the underwear in the interest of efficiency. When he had to empty his bladder, timing was crucial, and he didn't want to fumble around with extra material.

"What do you think?" Paul asked.

"Knowing you, and your sudden need to cover up, I would say no."

Paul finally got the screen positioned just right, and I snapped it into place. He ran the shaver over his face and began to look more like himself. He had missed two hairs on his upper lip, so I took them off with a straight razor, along with several long ones that had been dangling on his neck for weeks. I was struck by Paul's trusting pose as I aimed the razor just below his nose.

Afterward, I lay my head on his shoulder. "I'm tired," I said. "It's been a long week."

"I know," Paul said. "It shows a little bit. Just rest."

"I could fall asleep in two minutes," I said.

"Please do."

I rested for a few minutes, and then we decided to write a letter together.

"Are you sure you're not too tired?" Paul asked.

"No. Are you?"

"A little, but let's at least get started."

"How long could it take to write a thank-you note?" I said naively, pulling out my laptop.

An hour and a half later, we had composed fifteen lines. Paul reclined on the bed and dictated, while I typed. He stopped for long stretches, searching for just the right word. Then he'd forget where he was and ask me to read everything back to him. We were writing to his Sunday school class in South Carolina. He had specific individuals in mind and was anticipating how they would react to the letter. Paul was embarrassed, too, that the correspondence was so long overdue, but he didn't know how to explain this.

"A year ago, six months ago, three months ago, I thought I would get back to South Carolina and tell them in person how I felt," Paul said during one of his pauses. "Now I don't think I'll ever get there. I've had to accept that."

Paul was also distracted by a pain in his side, as well as the memory of how bad the pain had been the night before. He was holding his hand over the left side of his chest.

"What kind of pain?" I asked. "Heart pain? Did you tell the nurse?"

"It's not that kind of pain," Paul said. "It feels like a bruised rib."

We finally finished the letter, and Paul was enormously pleased.

"You have the patience of Job," he said. "I didn't think we'd get that much done."

Later, when I called him to say I'd gotten home all right and the door was locked, Paul said, "That was wonderful, what you did tonight. A little thing like sending a letter to friends means *everything*, because I may never see them again."

IN OUR time together, Paul and I perfected the cheap date: eating out only occasionally at family places (although once Paul insisted on going to White Castle, Detroit's signature hamburger joint, where he devoured several greasy burgers that made him queasy for two days); seeing matinees and second-run movies (we liked the Redford Theater, which ran classic films for $1.50 on Saturday nights and offered an old-time organ recital during intermission); driving around to see how much Detroit had changed in the last few years; visiting the farmer's market on a Saturday morning, just to observe the summer's bounty (it reminded Paul of all the plants he had nourished in his lifetime); browsing in bookstores; watching videos; reading newspapers and magazines together (I read aloud, while Paul listened and commented). One evening we even cruised the nursing home grounds together on his scooter.

Our biggest outing, a holiday concert at Orchestra Hall, required a shopping trip. Paul needed a pair of dress pants. We went to a men's store, and I accompanied Paul into the dressing room, where he tried on at least ten pair of pants, getting in and out of them very slowly and with great effort. I was appalled to discover that he hadn't put on a pair of underpants.

"You aren't supposed to try on clothes like that!" I gasped. "It's unhygienic!"

"Yes, but it's even more unhygienic when you pee all over yourself," Paul countered. "I need quick access to the waterworks. Underwear slows me down."

We didn't inform the manager about the indiscretion, but I'm sure the tailor could tell when he measured Paul for the alternations. Paul had selected cuffed, navy wool pants with deep, roomy pockets and a sharp crease. He was thrilled with the purchase. "For once I will be properly attired," he beamed.

ONE GLOOMY, boring Saturday morning, Paul went down to the dining room feeling lousy. He'd been up and down all night, in and out of the bathroom. Exhausted by the demands of his body, he shuffled down to breakfast about seven o'clock, nodded to his tablemates, surveyed the heavy oatmeal, and sighed. Too sleepy for eating or socializing, he took a few sips of weak coffee and returned to his room. He had just settled into his chair for a nap when the activities director came in to remind him that the high school band concert was tomorrow afternoon.

"Can I bring a guest?" Paul asked, seizing the opportunity for a date.

"I guess that would be all right, " she said. "We could probably squeeze another person onto the bus."

"I'll do the squeezing," Paul said. "You just worry about finding a seat for her." Then he called me.

"If there was a concert tomorrow, would you be able to go to it?" he asked.

"I might," I said, doing a quick mental survey of my work schedule. "Where and what time?"

"I don't know, exactly," Paul said. "I'll have to call you back."

He hung up and walked down to the activities room to get the specifics, but the director wasn't around. He returned to his room and fell asleep. He was awakened three hours later by a voice on the loud speaker: "THE LOCATION OF THE BAND CONCERT HAS BEEN CHANGED FROM THE HIGH SCHOOL GYMNASIUM TO THE CIVIC CENTER AUDITORIUM. THE BUS WILL LEAVE IMMEDIATELY AFTER LUNCH." An aide knocked on the door to alert Paul that it was time for lunch. He felt a rush of panic. How could he possibly get ready for the concert in time? He still had to shave and get his shoes and socks on. He was shaking badly now and feeling even worse. He called me again.

"They say the bus is leaving right after lunch, and I'm not ready."

"Wait," I said, trying to shift gears. "I thought you said the concert was tomorrow."

"What day is today?" Paul asked.

"Saturday."

"The concert is Sunday," Paul said, "but they just announced something that makes me think it might be today."

"Well, I'm not ready to go today. You'll have to go without me."

96

"I don't feel like it anyway," Paul said, defeated by the sheer effort of planning.

"See if you can find out for sure what day the concert is," I suggested, already feeling guilty. "And call me back."

Paul hung up, anxious and confused. He went down to the dining room, where they were serving roast beef, mashed potatoes, and green beans, all his favorites. It was the best lunch they'd served since he'd moved in, but he couldn't enjoy it. He got up three times during the meal to search for the activities director. Finally, he gave up, went back to his room, and collapsed in his chair.

When I called, he was taking another nap. "I've just called the activities director and determined that the concert is tomorrow, and the bus leaves at 1:30," I reported. "So relax and enjoy your nap. You don't have to do a thing this afternoon. You have a whole day to get ready."

"Thank you, honey, that's such a relief. But it's lonely as hell around here. If you feel like it today, could you pass by my room and blow me a kiss?"

"I don't think so, Paul, especially if I'm coming tomorrow," I said. "I've got to get this grant proposal done. Besides, how can you be lonely with all those women watching and hanging on your every word?"

"Ah, this happy nest of birds," Paul sighed. "And my little thrush, out in the swamp alone. I ache for you."

I hung up and went back to work, but pretty soon I was directing my car toward his side of town.

PAUL HAD mentioned several times that he'd like for us to go to church together. He had been an active member of the United Methodist Church in South Carolina and greatly missed the church community. One Saturday night in late January, I called and invited him to attend church with me the next morning. I had looked in the phone book and found a Methodist church within five miles of the nursing home.

"Oh, yes, let's go," Paul said enthusiastically. "I'm glad you thought of it."

"The service starts at eleven," I said. "But I'll be there at ten to give us enough time to get there. We should probably take your twelve o'clock meds, because we won't be back until 12:30 or so. Do you mind being late for lunch?"

"No, that will be fine. Whatever you say, dear."

The next morning, I called at 9:15 to tell Paul I was on my way.

"How was your night?" I asked, trying to determine his health status. "Do you still feel like going?"

"What's the matter, are you trying to get out of it?" Paul asked.

"No, I'm just making sure you're up for it."

"I just got back from breakfast. I'm all ready except for a few last-minute things. I have to shave and comb my hair."

"OK, then," I said, relieved. "I'll see you in forty-five minutes."

I arrived to find Paul holding a pair of pants and trembling.

"I'm sorry, honey," he said. "I wanted to be ready. But I also wanted to change my pants and put on a pair with a crease in them. So I told the head woman in the laundry room that I was going to church, and would they run an iron over my pants? I reminded her that the nursing home director had agreed during my last care conference that I could have my pants pressed. But she wouldn't hear of it. 'Oh, no,' she said. 'We don't press anything. Just wear these,' and she handed me these, which are nice pants with a cuff, but they aren't pressed. She was afraid she'd have to do the ironing and got me off the topic as quickly as possible. So then I tried to put these on, but I was getting shaky by then, and there's never an aide in sight when you need one. I needed socks, too, and I couldn't find any until I finally looked under the bed. So now I have two socks and a pair of wrinkly pants, but I'm afraid I'm not going to be ready in time." While recounting these events, Paul had started to tremble even more.

I assured him that we still had plenty of time and that I would help him dress. I unbuttoned and unzipped the cotton pants Paul was wearing. As they fell to the floor, Paul looked confused and started pulling them up again.

"Are we taking these off or putting them on?" I asked.

"I thought I was putting them on."

"But you said you wanted to put on the other ones," I countered.

"Oh, I haven't done that yet?" Paul said, pulling his pants down again.

When we finally had the second pair on, we spent another five minutes looking for his belt, which had fallen off the back of Paul's recliner.

"I'm sorry," Paul said weakly. "You didn't bargain for this."

"It's OK, Paul," I said hastily, eyeing my watch. "But now we have to hustle." I still had to get Paul outside and into the car, drive to the church, get Paul out of the car, usher him into the church over snowy sidewalks, and find us both a seat in a crowded church.

"My whole schedule is off this morning," Paul complained. "As you know, timing is everything with this medication. They got me up before six to give me my pills, which was too early. I set them aside for a little bit and then decided to take them anyway. But it's too long a time until the next pills. I'm already feeling shaky. Plus I got out of bed this morning, and my knee wouldn't work. Buckled underneath me. Now it hurts like hell."

"Paul, we don't have to go, you know. If you don't feel like it, just say so."

"But you look so pretty. How can you possibly want to go out with an old mess like me?"

"I want to go if you do."

"Just pour me in the river on your way to the church."

"Why are you talking like that?" I said, getting frustrated now.

"I'm just releasing steam, honey." Paul said. "Must I wear an overcoat?"

"It's twenty degrees outside! Why don't you want to wear a coat?"

"Because it's so much trouble, putting it on, taking it off, getting in and out of the car in it."

"It's definitely too cold to go without one, so we're putting it on. Let's get the pills and sign you out."

Convincing the nurse to give us the pills took another ten minutes. Paul took mincing steps down the hall toward the elevator, coming to a dead stop once or twice and then tripping forward.

"Where's the lady who monitors the door?" Paul asked when we got to the elevator.

"Paul, she's on the first floor. We're still on the second floor." I was starting to worry now.

"I knew that. Well, I didn't, but I do now. Don't worry, I'll wake up eventually."

I had parked as close as possible to the front door, but it took Paul a long time to get into the car.

"Heck," he said. "They're gonna find me still here at lunchtime."

The drive to the church took another ten minutes. I dropped Paul off at the door and parked the car. Once inside, we found the lobby crowded with people and with kids running around selling donuts for a bake sale.

"Shall we take your pills now or wait until afterward?" I asked. Paul had already forgotten about the pills.

"Oh. How about one now and one later?" he suggested. We found a drinking fountain, and I fished the pills out of my purse. By then, both of us had to use the bathroom.

We took our seats just as the service began. The single pill kicked in about fifteen minutes later, and Paul's tremor subsided. After that, things went more smoothly. Following the service, Paul sailed out the door and into the car. The fog in his mind seemed to have lifted, too.

"I'm sorry for all the inconvenience," Paul said as we drove back to Bedford.

"Let's look on the bright side," I suggested. "You're teaching me to accept the things I can't control."

Paul was pensive for a moment. "I must have done something good in my life to deserve you."

"I think you did—and still do—many good things."

"I never want to keep you from your other plans," Paul said gently.

"What could be more important than spending time with someone you love?"

"That's true. There's nothing truer," Paul said.

7 PASSION'S PROGRESS

Within four or five months, Paul and I were talking on the phone or seeing each other every day. Paul couldn't go to sleep without saying goodnight.

PAUL: I just called to say I love you. I won't keep you long. You're some kind of woman.

RUTH: Thank you. And you're some kind of man. I was just thinking about you.

PAUL: I know. That's why I called. It's mental telepathy. You'll find it itemized on your phone bill.

RUTH: I think about you a lot. It's hard to get my work done. I don't want to write a scholarly book. I want to write a love story!

PAUL: Well, get to it, baby.

RUTH: I suspect we're writing it now.

PAUL: Yes, we surely are.

Unlike many men who say what they think women want to hear, Paul meant what he said. And he didn't play games.

One day when Dan came to the nursing home for Paul's care conference, he walked into Paul's room and said, "Dad, you're looking damn good!"[1]

"Thank you," Paul said. "I'm in love."

At the conference, Paul requested that the nurses bring his pills on time, that he get an extra banana at meals, and that his pants be ironed. When he had first moved in, he had argued for an iron of his own. "I wanted to be able to press my own britches," Paul told me. "I had one in the old place, but they wouldn't let me bring it over here. I like to wear nicely creased pants that fit, not these old baggy wash clothes." The director of nursing wouldn't allow Paul his own iron, but she did agree to have the laundry iron a pair of pants now and then.

After the conference, Paul pulled Dan aside. "I meant what I said about Ruth. She's a wonderful woman, and I love her."

As he was leaving, Dan said, "I'm happy for you, Dad." Dan put his hand in his back pocket and said, "I meant to give my boy some date money."

It is a fact that, even in old age, Paul attracted women. Two or three still called from South Carolina, and those in the nursing home, even the demented ones, regularly tried to get Paul's attention. He was always telling me stories about women's advances, usually in the context of some other event.

"What's the name of that guy who sits in the lobby by the front door?" Paul asked me one day when I was visiting.

"Martin? Martin Stacy?"

"Right. The guy with two first names."

"What about him?"

"He died last night. Just like that, dead and gone."

"I just talked to him the other day," I said. "He seemed like a nice man. Did he and Hester, the woman with Alzheimer's from our writing group, have a thing going on?"

"Yes, you could say so. And it got him into a lot of trouble," Paul said. "He has a wife, a terrible, mean, bossy woman, who lives on the dementia unit. She'd come down the hall, and people would warn him: 'Here she comes!' and he'd drop Hester's hand like a hot potato. His wife would lay into him. He'd be all defensive with 'we didn't' and 'I never,' stumbling all over himself."

"Really?" I said. "And what about Hester? How did she react?"

"Hester is a hussy!" Paul said.

"What? That's a strange thing to say!"

"One time I saw her—and nobody saw this but me—I was coming around the corner of the dining room. That noisy corner in the old Bedford near the kitchen. She and I were the only ones in the room. Her dress was gaping open, and you could see her breasts. Well, actually, they were *tits*, so long you could step on 'em. She looked at me and pulled one of those out and slapped it on the table. She started rubbing it with a paper towel, back and forth, like it was a barber's strap. I said, 'Don't do that!' in a low, stern voice. She looked at me kind of guilty and put it back in her dress."

From Paul and the other residents, I was learning that sexuality is an important aspect of the human experience that continues into old age. But even when residents are physically able and desirous, there are many barriers to sexual expression in nursing homes, including lack of privacy; lack of available partners; negative attitudes of staff, physicians, and family members; and a general lack of knowledge about sexuality in old age.

ONE SUNDAY afternoon when I was visiting Paul in his room, the telephone rang. It was Mayleen from South Carolina. I listened to Paul's end of the conversation.

"Hello, darlin'. Thanks so much for the pecans. I had some and gave some to Dan's family. They were wonderful. How've you been?"

All very southern and civilized. Still, I felt a twinge of jealousy, and I asked Paul about her when they hung up.

"She's one of several women in South Carolina, members of Lila's Sunday school class and bridge club. They all keep in touch, but Mayleen has implied that she'd like to pursue a relationship. 'Why don't you come down here and take me out to dinner?' she says. All these women are widows. They have beautiful homes, and they're good cooks. But I don't want to marry any of them."

"Why not?" I asked. "I need to assess my competition."

"You have no competition. They don't appeal to me and never have. Mayleen is a very good woman, a do-gooder. I've never had any relations with her other than a friendly hello and a peck on the cheek as a greeting. But she writes about once a month, and she always ends with, 'I love you very much.'"

The female residents at Bedford made suggestive remarks to Paul all the time. Viola, who sat at the next table, said once, "I've got a box of chocolates in my room, Paul. Drop by for a piece any time." When that didn't work, she got more assertive. As she wheeled into the dining room one morning, she said, "Paul! Kiss me, I'm coming!"

"I'm the main stud in this stable," Paul said of his place in the nursing home, "and I don't like it one bit."

"No?" I said. "I thought all men liked to be considered studs."

"But I'm a quiet, discreet man," Paul said. "I don't like all this attention."

"Did something happen recently?"

"It happens all the time. Yesterday, Eleanor blew me a kiss from her seat in the dining room. Then she thought about it and called out, 'That was just a friendly kiss, Paul!'"

Since nursing home residents are about 85 percent female, and among the small percentage of men, very few are lucid and mobile, much less single and attractive, the attention Paul drew from the ladies was inevitable. He was not only nice to look at, but he could hold up his end of a conversation, make jokes, and offer compliments.

Women had always been attracted to Paul. When Lila died, two or three of her best friends made it known that they were available. "They were lovely people," Paul said, "but I wasn't interested."

Paul had been married three times, a fact that surprised even him. His first wife, Iris, the mother of his three children, had died of breast cancer, but this was after their midlife divorce. His second wife, Jean, had been unfaithful, and Paul divorced her. Then he spent several years in his fifties as a bachelor in South Carolina. He rented a room from Lila and kept steady company with a nurse at the local hospital, where he worked as a groundskeeper. When he was nearing sixty, Lila asked Paul to marry her, and he agreed.

"One day she took me into the kitchen and pointed to the calendar. 'How about getting married on that day?' she suggested. And I said, 'OK, let's do it.'"

He took the nurse out for a steak dinner the next night and broke the news. She was angry and hurt. But Paul was making a practical decision. He had just been diagnosed with Parkinson's, and the nurse had a slight disability of her own. Paul thought they probably wouldn't be able to grow old together, and he might end up taking care of her. The nurse ran out of the restaurant in tears. Paul still felt bad about the way things ended.

"It worked out for the best, though," Paul reasoned. "Lila and I spent nearly twenty good years together, and we loved each other. I think I made her happy."

At the nursing home, even the female staff took a special interest in Paul. The day receptionist, a handsome German woman of about sixty, often brought Paul flowers from her garden. When she saw him in the hallway, she would graze his cheek with a kiss. The first time Dan witnessed this, his mouth flew open. Slightly embarrassed, Paul said, "I don't ask for it, Dan."

In the beginning, whenever I accompanied Paul through the front door, the German woman would greet him and ignore me. Later, she adopted a motherly attitude toward us both. The first time Paul and I walked out together on a Saturday afternoon and returned on a

Sunday morning, she looked over the top of her glasses and said with exasperation, "Oh, Paul! Are you just getting *home*?!"

As things heated up between Paul and me, attention in the nursing home increased, too.

The female residents on his wing seemed obsessed with Paul's comings and goings. On the Sunday Paul and I went to church, we walked into the dining room a little late for lunch, and the three women at the table behind us—Eleanor, Violet, and Rose—began whispering excitedly in loud tones. "He's wearing a dark blue coat!" Rose exclaimed to her tablemates. "He looks very distinguished," Eleanor said with admiration. After I had helped Paul off with his overcoat, Rose said breathlessly, "Oh! He's wearing a suit jacket!" as if she hadn't seen a well-dressed man in years. "They must have gone out somewhere," Violet said wistfully.

Mostly, the women focused on Paul, but once I overheard them talking about me. "I believe she's put on some weight," Violet said.

RUMORS ABOUT us ran rampant. While waiting for the breakfast trays one morning, Violet said to Paul, "I hear you're getting married."

"Nonsense," Paul said. "Where'd you hear that?"

"I was sitting at the nurses' station," Violet said. "And the aides were talking about it."

"They deal in speculation," Paul responded.

"She's very pretty," Violet offered.

"She's *beautiful*," Paul countered, "inside and out."

"I'm glad for you," Violet said. "Everybody needs someone to love."

Paul reported these conversations later on the phone. He was good at keeping me informed of the staff's and residents' reactions to our developing relationship, including the negative, the positive, and the unarticulated.

One afternoon, Paul was riding down the hallway in his scooter. An aide pulled him aside as he rounded a corner.

"Mr. Paul, how you doin' today?" she asked.

"Fine, thank you."

"Is that girl your daughter or is she really your girlfriend?"

"I thought we'd already been through this," Paul said politely.

"Yeah, but I don't know if you were kidding or not," the young woman said.

"She's a nice woman and a good friend," Paul said.

"Well, uh, can you, uh . . ."

"What are you trying to say?" Paul asked. "Spit it out."

The aide giggled. "I was wondering if you could, well, if you were . . ."

"I don't know why you are having so much trouble speaking today," Paul said evenly. "Talk to me again when you get your thoughts formulated." And he spun off down the hall.

After a few more of these exchanges, the aides gave up the search for details. But every alert person at Bedford seemed aware of our relationship.

One day a man from another wing, whom Paul had never met, stopped him in the hallway and said, "I hear you have a much younger girlfriend."

"Yes," Paul confirmed.

"I wish you luck with that," the man said and shook his hand.

The nurses and the administrators were politely interested. Grace, one of our favorite nurses, was downright encouraging. She was fiftyish, good-natured, and plainspoken. Periodically she would ask Paul, "Are you and your girlfriend still together? Are you going to get married? What's stopping you? If you love each other, why not?"

Paul would answer in his pleasantly evasive way. "Yes, we're still together, but we're keeping our options open. There's much to be said for glorious freedom, you know!"

IT WAS difficult for us to find any privacy in this environment, even though Paul had a private room. Anyone who lives in a nursing home will tell you the place is buzzing with activity day and night.

First, there are the residents who don't mean to bother you but who are incredibly bothersome.

Paul called one such woman the "wolf lady," because she sometimes howled. She parked her wheelchair in the middle of the hallway and tried to get people's attention.

"Hep me, hep me," she'd say in her Kentucky accent.

"What do you want, Celia?" an aide would ask.

"You're up there, and I'm down here, and I want to go up there. Come git me."

Celia had a tremor in her left hand, which she held up in the air away from her. It looked like she was constantly waving you down. Celia was also a door-knocker. One evening when I was visiting Paul, we closed his door for a little more privacy. Immediately, there was a knock. When I opened the door Celia said, "Are you the lady of the house? I'd like to know where to deliver these goods."

Paul didn't find these interruptions amusing. The next day, he told the charge nurse, "If Celia knocks on my door again, I'm going to turn a fire hose on her!" Not that he *had* a fire hose, but he relished the thought of it.

Then there were the aides and nurses and housekeeping staff who came and went, in and out of Paul's room, day and night.

Once Paul and I were lying on his bed with the door closed, kissing and joking around. Paul tugged on his shirt, attempting to pull it out of his pants.

"Put your hand on my chest," he said. I unbuttoned his shirt and began to rub his chest and stomach. Paul closed his eyes and smiled dreamily.

"How is that sore on your back?" I asked.

"Still there. I wanted you to look at it again when you had time."

I pushed him into an upright position and pulled up his shirt to inspect the middle of his back.

"It's about an inch long, it's round, and it has a scab on it," I reported.

109

"Give it to me straight," Paul said. "It's a bullet wound, isn't it?"

I laughed. "I don't think you caught a bullet at Bedford Continuing Care."

"A .22 got me in the hallway. It was a jealous suitor. He was a bad shot, though, and he only grazed me. That's why there's no bullet hole."

"More likely a bedsore, partly healed," I said. "We'll keep an eye on it."

"Thank you, darlin'," Paul said.

I continued rubbing Paul's back. He leaned against me and sank into the massage.

"You make my body smile all over," he purred. "It's funny how things come around. All these years, this is what I've wanted, a woman to touch me lovingly. All this time, and now . . ."

There was a knock on the door. I hastily buttoned up my blouse, while Paul threw a blanket over himself.

"Come in," Paul said.

An aide opened the door and flipped on the overhead light.

"Oh, I—" she faltered. "You have a telephone call at the nurses' station."

"Who is it?" Paul asked.

"Your sister, Mary Ann," the aide said.

"Well, I'll be darned," Paul, said. "Tell her I'll call her back. I'm not feeling well right now. I didn't sleep last night."

"She wants to know if she can have your direct number," the aide said.

"Yes, yes, of course," Paul said. By now, he had gotten up to look through the pile of business cards and slips of paper for his own telephone number.

"In the interest of time," Paul said. "Get her telephone number and tell her I'll call back."

The aide left the door slightly ajar on her way out. Paul pulled his clothes together. "She'll be back any minute," he said.

The aide knocked again and brought Paul the telephone number.

"She says she's sorry you're not feeling well and she'll talk to you soon," the aide reported.

"Thank you, dear," Paul said.

The aide closed the door on her way out but left the overhead lights on.

"This is really an awful situation," I growled. "I can't stand this lack of privacy."

Paul listened and said, "I guess I'm used to it."

There was another knock on the door.

"Come in," Paul said.

A different aide entered, picked up Paul's plastic urinal, which was hanging on the edge of the wastebasket, and emptied it into the toilet. She left without a word.

"I wonder how she knew that needed emptying?" Paul said.

"I think she just wanted to spy," I said irritably.

We talked some more and began kissing again. This time there was a rattling of the doorknob first. Paul and I flew apart. I sat up and smoothed my hair.

A woman from housekeeping walked into the room without knocking.

"Sorry, I didn't know you had company," she said offhandedly. "I was going to vacuum your room, but I could come back." She left with the wastebasket in her hand.

"She didn't even knock!" I sputtered.

"She didn't?"

"No! That was rude and insensitive. I feel like a guilty teenager, and I have nothing to feel guilty about!"

"Yes, this arrangement is not ideal," Paul admitted.

"Is it like this *all* the time?" I asked.

"Pretty much."

"I can see why you're sleep deprived! You have no assurance of uninterrupted time."

"I guess I didn't realize how bad it was," Paul said.

"Well, I'm here to tell you, Paul, this is *not* a private room! If you're paying extra for it, you should get your money back."

IN THE end, all we could do was laugh about the situation.

"Why don't you come over here so I can rub your back?" Paul would say on the phone.

"Great. I'll bring my toothbrush and spend the night!"

"No, wait! I'm chicken," Paul said.

"What are you afraid of? Some silly house rules? Prying eyes?"

"All of the above!"

"Wait, I know!" I said, making my voice breathless and excited. "I'll bring sleeping bags! We'll pitch a tent on the front lawn! That way, we can sleep together on the premises and still be on time for breakfast."

"Should I request that they deliver my tray to the tent flap?"

"No, that would be pushing our luck. We'll go to the dining room."

"I love it when you talk crazy!" Paul said.

8 ACTIVITIES

I was reading the *Detroit Free Press* aloud to Paul when we came across an article that perfectly described the mental state of a nursing home resident. It was about woodchucks, also known as groundhogs, marmots, or whistle dogs. The woodchuck falls into a state of inertia from late fall to spring, alternating between deep hibernation and periods of torpor.

"Tor—per," Paul said, enjoying the sound of the word. "I know it all too well."

After that, I called him "my little marmot," although the deadening tug of institutional life is not a laughing matter.

Paul was fine when I was visiting, or he was visiting me, or when Dan was around, but there are twenty-four hours in every day and an endless procession of days. Afternoons were the worst. Sometimes Paul would jack up his hospital bed as high as it would go and sit in the air for a while, just to get a different point of view. Then he'd stroll through the hallway a couple of times and maybe stop in the lobby to leaf through a magazine. He'd wander back to his room, plop down in the recliner, and flip through the TV channels. Paul kept the TV on constantly, a noisy backdrop to perpetual boredom.

"Tell me something about your day," I'd say over the phone in the evening.

"Phooey! That about covers it," he'd say. "Nothing ever happens. There's nothing to tell. Except now they're serving the cranberry juice in flat cartons instead of round plastic cups. How's that for news?"

The attempts of nursing home staff to liven things up, however well intended, only throw into relief the banalities of institutional life. The great equalizer in nursing homes is food, which is why "activities" usually center around it: heart-shaped cookies on Valentine's Day; red, white and blue cake and ice cream on the Fourth of July; pumpkin-shaped cookies with orange frosting on Halloween. In between, the staff grasps at any potential food event. At Paul's nursing home, they celebrated Fat Tuesday before Lent with paczki's—Polish donuts filled with jelly, fruit, or custard—even though few residents were Catholic or Polish, and nobody needed the extra fat and sugar.

Paul was roused from a nap one afternoon by an aide, asking if he wanted to come down to the dining room for "tea and toast."

"I couldn't imagine why I would want to eat toast at three o'clock in the afternoon," he reported, "so soon after the mound of wet food that had been served at lunchtime and an hour and a half before the next mound at dinnertime. I politely declined the invitation."

In their minimum data assessments, nursing home staff are required to document how much time each resident spends "in activity," as well as what kind of activity it is. It is therefore incumbent upon staff to create social situations that can be codified and counted. Unfortunately, as the gerontologist Steve Katz points out, staff-generated activities are comically inconsistent with the activities that naturally arise out of people's daily lives. If residents choose their own activities over the institutional ones, however, they may be considered a "problem," especially if the activities are internal and immeasurable, like thinking, meditating, and praying, or personal and private, like courting, cuddling, and engaging in sexual play. This is why Katz refers to residents under nursing-home rule as "busy bodies." The basic assumption underlying activities programs, he notes, is that "health" in America connotes an active, independent, utilitarian lifestyle; nursing home residents, however frail, ill, tired, or disinterested, are expected to "keep busy." From an institutional standpoint, the success of an activities program is the number of busy bodies participating in scheduled social events.[1]

What residents really need, say critics, is cultural acceptance that old age is a unique period in life that actually requires *less* social activity and more private introspection. Feminist critic Margaret Cruikshank considers prescribed busyness an "unimaginative expectation" for old people and a form of social control that reflects a general fear of old age. "Behind the busy ethic," says Cruikshank, "is the secret wish that midlife will extend indefinitely. Fear of the unknown and uncontrollable is natural, and attempts to ward it off through busyness understandable. But the inexorable process of change sweeps away our protective cover of busyness and deposits us, ready or not, at the border of old age."[2]

Most American nursing homes, dominated by a medical model of care that focuses on the physical body, fail to acknowledge the internal changes that occur in old age. The nursing home reformist and physician William Thomas argues that nursing home administrators must look to residents, rather than health care "experts" and gerontologists, to create environments that respond better to individual needs and desires, including an increased need for privacy. The problem with a resident's spending time alone is that health care professionals typically interpret such behavior as evidence of depression. Rather than experiencing a pathological state, however, the resident may in fact be entering into a final developmental stage. The gerontologist Lars Tornstam, calls this period "gerotranscendence" and describes it as a shift from a rationalist, materialist view of the world to a more cosmic, transcendent view that may entail decreased interest in superficial social interactions and an increased need for solitude and meditation.[3]

THE MOST popular activity at Bedford was the brainstorm of the residents council, not the activities director. It was a simple event with major impact. One Saturday a month, the residents participated in Crunchy Toast Day. On that morning, toasters were brought into the dining room and turned up to "brown." Resident volunteers lightly buttered the bread as soon as it emerged from the toasters, and aides distributed it immediately to assure the desired crunch. Every other day of the month, toast was served the institutional way: brushed with melted butter in the kitchen, placed on trays in a dinner cart, wheeled to the dining room, and left to sit until the aides could distribute the trays. Toast was reliably cold and soggy. Crunchy Toast Day was successful because it was proposed and executed by residents and because it arose from the desire for all to share in something that represented "normal" everyday life. The simple act of preparing toast allowed the female residents to play a small role in the production of food—something most had been doing all their lives as daughters, wives, mothers, and grandmothers. And the toast itself was a sensory reminder of life outside the nursing home.

Sometimes activities directors appeal to family members for help in developing activities. Here, for example, is a volunteer "wish list" from another nursing home I visited:

1. someone to direct the resident choir every other week
2. someone to conduct a Bible study group
3. materials for the sewing group, including cotton for quilts, used cotton flannel blankets, fabric scraps, leftover spools of thread, bits of lace, and fancy buttons

4. several people willing to visit one-on-one, read aloud, play cards, take walks, or just hold someone's hand

Unfortunately, these modest requests go unmet for months at a time. Scheduling is part of the problem. Nursing home activities generally occur in the middle of the day, between 10:00 and 11:00 a.m. or between 2:00 and 3:00 p.m., prime time for working people. The activities "staff," which often consists of one person, assumes most of the responsibility for creating a social environment in the nursing home. This person does what she can in the time available, but her options are limited, and the results are mixed. On the Bedford calendar for May 1997, for example, every Sunday morning was starred as a major social event: "Bagel Time!" "Donut Time!" "Muffin Time!" When I read these aloud to Paul, he snorted. "I'll show them muffin time!" he said, playfully grabbing at me.

The worst thing about scheduled events is that they leave no room for spontaneity. Indeed, the perfect activity for nursing home staff is one where everybody shows up but nothing really happens. This is true even of a party. For our first Valentine's Day together, I sent Paul a card and visited him that evening. Paul told me he had "walked on a cloud for hours" after receiving the card. He wanted to give me something, too, but he had no money and nowhere to spend it. He finally came up with two cookies and a few candy hearts with messages stamped on them ("Be mine," "U R Sweet,"), which he took from the Bedford Valentine's Day party and wrapped in a paper napkin. There were a lot of those hearts left over because no one could chew them.

"Tell me about the party," I said, sitting cross-legged on Paul's bed.

"How to describe a Bedford party?" he said, gearing up for a recitation. "I thought I might just look in on it, but I didn't want to stay long. I walked into the dining room, and an aide rushed up and said, 'Here's a chair for you, Mr. Mason. I've got a chair right here for you!' She was all excited because the other chairs were taken and she

117

had to pull one in from the lobby. One of those cushy upholstered chairs. They make such a fuss, it's ridiculous."

"They were thrilled to see you. They need all the men they can get at these affairs," I said.

"Sometimes these efforts—special treatments and so forth—can have the opposite effect," Paul said. "They can cause resentments in other people. I don't want to be treated differently."

"You felt singled out?"

"Precisely."

"So what happened next?"

"There was some woman there, trying to lead a sing-along."

"Did you sing?"

"I can't remember. If I did, I wasn't loud enough to hear myself." Paul was warming to the story now, so I raised one of our favorite subjects.

"Did they have anything good to eat?"

"I had a Coke, a couple of potato chips, some dry little thing—a cheese twisty doodle hoo of some sort. As soon as I finished, somebody ran up all breathless and said, 'Do you want some more?'"

We were both chuckling now. I went for more details, knowing there weren't any.

"Did they have a conversation hour after the entertainment?"

"Nope. Everybody sat around and looked at each other. Every time I geared up to say something to someone, the next thing I knew, he had turned to look the other way."

This made me laugh, because under most circumstances, Paul could hold a conversation with anyone.

"I drummed my fingernails on the table for a while, just to break the monotony. After a half hour or so, I said, 'Well, that's enough excitement for one day,' and I came back to my room. By that time, the nurses were here with the meds, passing out the cranberry juice."

I hooted at that. Cranberry juice was the punch line to our running joke on nursing home life.

"Now, *that's* the high point of my day," Paul said, grinning. "I love to hear you laugh."

EVERY ONCE in a while, Paul would make the mistake of treating the nursing home as a home. One morning he walked down to breakfast in his bare feet. An aide noticed immediately and said, "You don't have your shoes on, Mr. Mason."

"I know that," Paul said, pleasantly.

"But you have to wear shoes," she said.

"Why?" Paul asked.

"Because you could trip and fall on the carpet," she replied.

"It seems to me," Paul reasoned, "that my bare feet would give me a better understanding on this carpet than a pair of slippers with a smooth sole."

"Oh, no, we can't have that," the aide insisted. "We have rules and regulations, you know." She went to Paul's room and returned with his slippers.

"Here," she said, handing them to Paul.

"Put on your rules and regulations," Paul grumbled. "This place drives me crazy sometimes," he said to Morris. "They take something perfectly normal and turn it into a problem."

Later that morning, Paul tested his limits again. He walked into the hallway while running the electric razor over his face.

"What are you doing?" asked the nurse on duty.

"Shaving," said Paul.

"You're shaving? In the hallway?"

"Yes," Paul confirmed. "I'm shaving in the hallway."

"Well, I, we . . . why?" the nurse stammered.

"To get the whiskers off my face," Paul said mildly.

"I've never seen anyone shave in the *hall*," she said.

"I was selling tickets a few minutes ago," Paul said. "There was quite a crowd. But I'm all out now. You'll have to scrounge around and get a ticket from someone else. Watch out for scalpers!"

A male aide walked up to them and the nurse reported, "He's *shaving* in the *hall*!"

The young man recognized the humor in the situation and said, in mock concern, "Surely, you aren't *shaving* in the *hall*, Mr. Mason!"

"Yes," Paul said, "I am shaving in the hall. I don't see what all the commotion is about. When I was a young boy, just getting used to the world, the women would send my grandpa to the outhouse to shave. He had a big, thick, white beard. They'd say, 'And don't come out until you're clean!'"

When Paul reported this incident to me later on the phone, he said dryly, "Truly, I don't make this stuff up! The staff supplies the material. I just distribute it."

The nursing home ethnographer Nancy Foner explains that tensions between "home" and "institution" are bound to exist in the bureaucracies of capitalist societies. Drawing on the work of sociologists Max Weber and Anthony Giddens, Foner observes that "with its emphasis on strict adherence to rules and regulations, bureaucracy subverts the values of individuality, spontaneity and autonomy." While such adherence increases organization and efficiency, it inevitably depersonalizes care. Rules become an end in themselves and result in unthinking, inflexible behavior on the part of staff. Further, "because conformity to the rules is rewarded in bureaucratic organizations and deviations punished, the rules acquire a symbolic significance quite apart from their utility." The result is an "overzealous pursuit of efficiency" and an emotional detachment from the actual needs and desires of residents.[4]

To PASS the time in the afternoons, Paul engaged in flights of fancy. He especially relished the idea of going back to work. "Nothing too strenuous," he'd say. "I realize I have some limitations." He thought about selling motor homes to retirees. "I started doing that once," he said. "I could pick up that line of work again. There's a dealer out on M-59 that I could maybe talk into giving me a demonstration model."

"How are you going to get to work?" I asked, ever the pragmatist.

"I can't be bothered with facts," Paul responded. "I'm operating on hope. Besides, I could do much of the work from here, over the telephone."

Paul also had a business venture in the back of his mind called Eyepatch Enterprise. Paul wore a standard black cotton patch over his left eye socket. He figured that there were men all over the world, like him, who would like to have a little fun with an eyepatch. Paul already had the basic product line in mind. For business wear, he'd market the Daily Dress Patch made of a high-quality wool or wool blend in black and gray. The Workman's Patch would be made of denim, flannel, or a sturdy khaki material. For fun, he would sell a Party Patch, made of silk or satin.

"I know I couldn't get this business off the ground by myself," Paul said. "I would be the idea man, but I would need someone positive and enthusiastic—an enterprising youth—to work with me and build up a clientele. It takes just the right person for this kind of venture."

I didn't much like Paul's imaginary ad campaign. I considered it retrograde in its sexual politics, and I thought it objectified women. Paul argued that it was sensual, not sexual; that it appealed to a heterosexual man's aesthetic (my words, not his); and that it would successfully sell the product.

For the Party Patch advertisement, he envisioned a dark velvet backdrop with two single images in the foreground: a red silk eyepatch resting lightly on a milky white thigh.

9 DIAPER IS A DIRTY WORD

Bran flakes
Milk (whole)
Orange juice (canned is fine)
Two fried eggs (brown lace around the edges)
Two pieces toast (white or wheat)
Coffee

Paul and I had planned the breakfast menu for his first overnight visit.

"That would be a perfect breakfast," Paul had said. "But anything you want to fix is fine."

When I arrived on Saturday afternoon to pick him up, Paul had already packed his electric shaver, a comb, toothbrush, pajamas, a plastic urinal, and a bed pad with a quilted cotton top and a waterproof backing ("just in case I don't wake up in time," Paul said). He didn't have an overnight bag, so he'd put the items in a plastic grocery bag.

We needed enough pills for that night and the next morning until lunchtime. Fortunately, the good nurse was on duty—the open-minded one who kept asking when we were getting married.

She put Paul's pills in little envelopes and marked on the front the time he was supposed to take them.

"Have fun!" she said.

Another nurse, just leaving her shift, walked up and said, "Be good!"

"Well, it depends on what you consider being good," the first nurse said.

I HAD planned to serve steak for dinner. Having been a vegetarian for a while, though, I wasn't sure how to cook it. I asked Paul to oversee the process, and he took over entirely.

"I used to do this all the time in South Carolina," he said. "Lila would say to her son, 'Don't touch the steak. Paul will do that.' I used to clean up as I went along, so there wouldn't be a big mess at the end."

I was standing next to the stove making a salad. I watched Paul turn the burner on high and put a couple of inches of water in a cast iron skillet to season it, then pour out the water and put the steak in.

"Don't you want to put some oil in first?" I asked.

"Oh, yes, that was water I poured out," Paul said. He put vegetable oil in the skillet, let it get hot, and then plopped the steak in with a sizzle. The oil popped and bounced all over the stove.

"Are you sure you want the heat that high?" I asked warily.

"Yup," Paul said confidently. He struggled to turn the steak over with a fork, knocking a bottle of steak sauce on the floor. When the steak had browned on both sides, he tried to cut off a corner piece for a taste, but he was using a table knife.

"I thought you said you were giving me a steak knife," Paul said.

"I did, but I put it on the table next to your plate."

It didn't matter much anyway, because Paul couldn't chew the steak with his new dentures. He sucked on a piece or two and spit them out.

"Delicious," he said.

Both exhausted, we went to bed early. We propped ourselves up on pillows, and I read aloud to Paul. He fell asleep several times, waking each time and asking me to continue. We talked and kissed and snuggled. Paul slept in fits and starts of about twenty minutes at a time. On the nightstand, he had noticed my Voyager Galaxy, a battery-operated "learning and relaxation system" that was attached to a tape player. Its purpose was to trigger changes in your brain waves. The mechanism was the size of a handheld radio and came with twelve preset options, each of which emitted a different combination of pulsating lights and sounds, depending on whether you wanted to improve your focus, relax, meditate, catnap, or sink into a deep sleep. I put the earphones on Paul, and he enjoyed it immensely, although it didn't make him sleep any better.

"I like your dream machine," Paul said groggily.

We left a night light on so that he could see to use the urinal. I had assumed he could do this on his own, but time proved me wrong. Every hour and a half or so, Paul would say, "I gotta pee." I would throw off the covers, and he would inch himself over the side of the bed. Then he would slowly slide his legs over the edge and sit up, inching forward so that he could plant his feet on the floor. The first time he reached for the urinal and used it, he commented, "I've been so concerned about flushing the toilet when I went to the bathroom so you wouldn't hear me. Now I'm bringing it right in front of your nose." When he finished, he'd have to reverse the process to get back into a sleeping position. Getting up, using the urinal, and lying down again took him nearly ten minutes.

Around 2:30, Paul woke me up, his voice urgent. "I gotta pee, and I gotta go bad." This time, I got up and walked around to his side of the bed to pull him into a sitting position. He fumbled with his pajama bottoms. "It's coming," he said. "I'm too late. There's nothing

I can do." I grabbed the urinal and positioned it, but the flow had stopped by then. In the semidarkness, I saw that Paul's pajamas were wet, and there was a small puddle on the carpet. I got a warm, soapy washcloth and a towel from the bathroom. I helped Paul off with his pajamas and washed him.

"I never thought I would see your beautiful body bending over me doing something like this," Paul said. "I'm truly sorry. I got overconfident and allowed myself to fall asleep. I should have been just dozing."

We draped the waterproof pad over the side of the bed this time and put the towel on top of it, in case of future accidents. When we got back under the covers, Paul said, "I feel so degraded."

"Please don't," I said, trying to assure him. "These things happen."

"I asked my doctor if there was anything I could do, and he said there was nothing except a catheter, and those cause infections. But I'm going to consult with a doctor about how to get this garden hose working again."

"Is that how you're going to talk about it?" I asked, smiling in the dark.

"No," Paul said. "We'll discuss it man to man—when I get my courage up, that is. For now, I'm going to focus on getting up in time and peeing by myself. Just wait and see, mommy, I can do it all by myself!"

"That's a good boy," I said, patting his head.

"Every now and then, the nurses give me an extra pill," Paul said. "Ditropan, which I know is a water pill. I don't know why they get it in their heads that I need it. I've told them I don't want those ever again. I don't need them, because I have no trouble urinating. My problem is holding it *in*. 'All right, I'll look into it, Mr. Mason,' the nurse says. And then a few days later, there's the extra pill again!

"A week or so ago," Paul continued, "after I'd taken that damn pill, I was up all night and spent the day in the bathroom. I walked down to dinner, and halfway through the meal, I felt the urge to go.

I got up and walked toward the bathroom in the dining room, but I was moving too slow. I got just inside the door and lost control before I could get my pants down. I opened the door just a crack and tried to get the attention of that pudgy lady at the table next to mine. 'Is the aide around?' I asked. 'Tell her I want to see her.'

'Mary, Mr. Mason wants to see you,' she called out, motioning toward the bathroom.

Mary came up to the door, and I asked her to bring my wheelchair over and stand in front of the door while I got in, so the others wouldn't see my pants. Then I said, 'Get me the hell out of here!' And she whizzed me down the hall to my room.

"How embarrassing!" I said. "I'm sorry you had to go through that."

"I wasn't going to tell you about it, but here I am, confessing the whole thing. It was a terrible day. I felt lower than a fart in a gale."

I laughed at the comparison. "I don't think any less of you, Paul."

"Are you sure?"

"Yes."

"I feel much better just talking about it. This is a major problem for older people. I used to lie awake at night, trying to think up different contraptions to keep a person dry. This was after the aides started suggesting I wear diapers, at least during the night. But for me, that was not an option, at least not yet. Diaper is a dirty word, you know. As long as you can talk, anyway."

Paul's assessment that incontinence (accidental leakage of urine) seriously affects the quality of life for many older adults was accurate. According to the U.S. National Kidney and Urologic Diseases Information Clearinghouse, urinary incontinence affects an estimated 17 percent of men and 38 percent of women age sixty and older. Up to 90 percent of men in their seventies and eighties have enlarged prostates, the symptoms of which mirror Paul's—frequent urination, especially at night, urgency, and dribbling. Various diseases of the nervous system, such as Parkinson's, can also cause incontinence.[1]

When we returned to Bedford late the next morning, the German receptionist eyed us over the top of her glasses, but she didn't say anything. We stopped by Paul's room to drop off his plastic overnight bag. We looked at the pot of crocuses sitting on the windowsill and agreed that they had grown at least an eighth of an inch since yesterday.

Everyone else was already seated in the dining room, eating Sunday dinner. Eyes turned in our direction.

"I'll leave you to it," I said to Paul, touching his arm goodbye.

Paul reported the events to me later on the phone. The pudgy lady (Violet) had come over to his table and said, "Have you set a date yet?" Paul smiled but didn't say anything. Dan came to visit later in the afternoon, and Paul told him about the steak dinner and the sleepover.

"That's nice, Dad," Dan said. "I'm glad for you."

"I need some money to pay her back for that dinner," Paul said.

Dan patted his back pocket. "I was going to give you some money, but I forgot my wallet."

Paul gave him a look of mock disgust. Then he said, impulsively, "We'd like to get together with you and Susan for lunch or dinner to discuss our options."

"Oh?" Dan said, raising his eyebrows. "OK then."

"Ruth hasn't even met Susan yet," Paul said.

"May I have her telephone number?" Dan asked.

"Yes, of course," Paul said. "She asked me already to give it to you. But use it only for emergencies, OK?"

That evening and the next day, Paul overheard a low buzz in the hallways around the subject of "Paul and his girlfriend." A day nurse came up to him in the hall and said, "Paul, I hear you have a girlfriend. Is it serious?"

"Well, it might be," Paul said.

"Good for you," she said. "Everybody needs someone to love."

An aide, the one Paul called "the smart-alecky one," came up to Paul at lunch, leaned her elbows on the table and said, "So, did *you* have a good time this weekend?"

"Now, look here," Paul said. "This is a wonderful woman. Wipe that smirk off your face, and you might get an answer to your question."

The aide sobered up.

"I went to her house, and she made a delicious steak dinner," Paul said. "And that's enough excitement for one day."

Paul tried to focus on the positive comments, but later in the day, be began to feel uneasy. He kept hearing the smirky girl's voice, "Is she your girl? Is she *still* your girl?" Then another voice, his own, said, "Is she going to stick with you? Why should she?" He felt like crying. He called me at home and left a message on the machine.

"Hello, Ruthie dear. This is your old friend, Paul. I just want to say that if you need time to think, we could meet in a day or two. I just needed to hear your voice today, if only off a machine. I'm not going to call you again. I love you."

Later that night on the phone, we talked about Paul's blue mood and what people had been saying. I had called my mother, who was seventy-eight, and told her I had had "a few dates" with an eighty-two-year-old man I had met in a nursing home.

"You're kidding!" she said. "You'll try anything! Nothing you do surprises me." Then she paused and said, "It's not serious, is it? What would you want with an old man?"

"I like him very much," I said and changed the subject.

I had also emailed a friend in Boston and talked to a trusted colleague, a geriatric social worker, about my fondness for Paul. I received nothing but support and encouragement.

"I have an advantage over you, Paul," I said. "I have more people to talk to about this, and they are thoughtful, educated people with a broad perspective on things."

"Yes, I was going to mention this to you," Paul said. "I have no one to reveal any of my concerns and feelings to. I can talk to Dan about some of it, but not all of it."

"You need a close friend," I said. "But there aren't any nearby."

"I don't ask for a lifetime with you, or even a long time," Paul said. "Just the freedom to enjoy whatever time we have together. I wish I could protect you and make you feel secure in this world. I know I can't do it, but I want to."

"The very fact that you *want* to makes me feel secure," I said.

"I don't know how long I have to live," Paul said. "Going doesn't bother me so much, but I don't like the idea of leaving you to the wolves. I don't like it *one bit*."

"I think you worry too much about those wolves," I replied. "I don't see any wolves circling."

"There are always wolves around a good woman. They're just keeping their distance at the moment. It bothers me. You deserve a man of substance who will be completely devoted to you. There are very few of those around. Most men are wolves."

"Or babies who want mommies," I added. "I don't know which is worse."

"I wish I could do something about it," Paul fretted.

"OK, here's your assignment," I suggested. "When you leave, your job is to watch over me from wherever you are and keep me on track. If you spot a man of substance, point him out to me, and make me pay attention."

"A sign," Paul said.

"Yes. I'll wait for your sign. I won't do anything until I hear from you."

"That was a true lover's speech," Paul sighed contentedly. "And I thank you for it. As surely as I'm sitting here, I will give you a sign when the right man comes along."

IO CARE CONFERENCE

Paul had said he wanted me to meet Susan, so he arranged for us all to have dinner at a nearby restaurant. Susan and Dan arrived at the nursing home around four o'clock on a Saturday afternoon to pick us up for an early dinner. They rushed into Paul's room, already feeling stressed over the babysitter not calling to say she was running late, Susan's father just having gotten out of the hospital, and Dan having to work that day. We immediately piled into the car and headed for the restaurant.

Once there, we made small talk about work and family and skirted around the subject of politics. "At least you're both Democrats," Dan said, assessing Paul's and my compatibility. Dan himself was a small businessman and an ardent Republican. He referred to supporters of President Bill Clinton as "FOCs."

Paul had forgotten his glasses, so I read the menu aloud to him. He always selected the most delicious food he could find that he would never get in a nursing home. That day it was spare ribs. They were messy and hard to eat, but he didn't care. During dessert, I excused myself and went to the restroom. I returned to find Paul and Dan deep in conversation.

"This woman is one of a kind, and I love her," Paul was saying. "I can't say that enough to you, and the words don't express the feeling. She's kind and warm. She's direct and honest. She's smart. She's accomplished. And she accepts me as I am. I can't tell you what that means to me. There's no one more surprised than me that she's chosen to be with me. And I want to be with her, in whatever way I can."

Susan's face grew soft at Paul's words. Dan listened carefully and looked pensive. Paul went on to talk about the importance of romance and sharing his life with someone.

"I want a normal life in a real home!" he said, emphatically.

Of course, I had known this, but the statement brought me up short. What was Paul saying, exactly? We hadn't talked about sharing a home. I jumped into the conversation, trying to assuage Dan's fears, and my own, without contradicting Paul.

"Paul's the romantic in this duo," I said. "And I'm the pragmatist. I have many of the same concerns that you do, Dan, in terms of Paul's medical care and health benefits and whether he can get back into the nursing home if he leaves. We haven't made any decisions yet, and we won't act rashly. You will be involved all along the way. If we should decide to live together, we will hire an aide to assist Paul during the day."

This last comment surprised Paul. "A babysitter?" he said, looking at me.

"No," I corrected. "A companion, for my own peace of mind when I'm at work."

Dan was watching us intently. "It seems there are some things you haven't talked about," he said. "Ruth doesn't seem as enthusiastic about your moving in as you are, Dad. And what kind of arrangement would this be, anyway? Are you thinking about living together or getting married?"

"We haven't made any plans, Dan," Paul said. "Right now, we're just exploring our options."

But the conversation didn't feel that way to me. Paul was speaking with great force, carried away with the effort of explaining his hopes and dreams. As his words piled up, I began to see my independence pass before my eyes. I experienced a rush of panic.

Dan was talking about the need to do some fact-finding with government agencies. "What do you want me to do, Dad?" he asked. "Shall I talk to people for you or go with you?"

"Thank you, Dan," Paul said. "But I don't need a business manager. We want to do this ourselves."

"Well, " said Dan. "I can't stand in your way. You're adults. I want to be part of this and support you, if it's the right thing to do."

"We only want what's right for both of us," Paul said.

Susan didn't say much, but her face conveyed a range of emotions as the conversation progressed—surprise, curiosity, concern.

"My questions are medical and economic," Dan explained. "You've done so much better since moving to the nursing home, Dad. You've reached some stability in your health. I don't know if we should disrupt that. I thought you were getting used to being there, even liking it. I'm trying to understand your motivations here. I know you want some independence and a break from the nursing home. Can't you just continue dating? Go to her house on weekends, take a vacation together once in a while? I'm not sure a move is necessary."

"I appreciate your concerns," Paul said. "Believe me, we've thought of all of them. And yes, I've grown accustomed to life at Bedford, but it's institutional life. I want a home and the stimulation of other people. I am more alone in that home than you realize. I want to be around the people I love. When you come and fix a little thing in my room, get the TV working better, lie down on my bed and take a nap, it buoys me. When Ruth comes and eats with me, talks, and laughs at my jokes, offers me her sweet lips, I'm flying for hours afterward."

"I understand that, Dad," Dan said softly.

"I don't want to die in a nursing home, son," Paul said. "I'm still capable of making my own decisions, and I'm going to make this one in consultation with this woman here."

I found myself watching Paul from a distance. I saw a thin, frail old man whose hands were trembling. The hair on the back of his neck was scraggly, and the barber had cut the rest of his hair too short, making his ears protrude. I noticed how he got off the topic with his stories and how they rambled on too long. I also saw a man fighting for his life.

Paul was looking down at his hands. "That's not Parkinson's, Dan, that's tension."

"What's the time frame for this decision?" Dan asked. "When do you want to make this move?"

"Yesterday," Paul said.

"Well—" I hesitated.

Paul jumped in. "This doesn't have a time frame to it. We haven't thought of it in those terms."

"Let Ruth give her answer," Dan said.

"You're talking about drab practicalities, Dan," Paul said. "The smaller things will work themselves out."

"I'm just trying to figure out how much time I have to talk to government officials and get more information," Dan responded.

"You don't have to schedule anything," Paul said. "Like I said, we don't need a manager."

"In answer to your question, Dan," I said, clearing my throat. "Just in terms of what's going on in my own life, a move couldn't occur until May, at the very least, as I have to travel in March and April."

"There, you've got weeks and weeks," Paul said.

Later in Paul's room as we replayed the dinner conversation, Paul spoke with animation. "I reached a new level of citizenship tonight," he said. "I even *feel* taller." He stood up to his full height and extended his chest to demonstrate his sense of accomplishment. "Dan didn't like to hear that I don't want him to manage every aspect of my life. He's been taking care of my affairs since I moved in here, and he's done a good job, but I will not allow him to make this decision for me. We are capable of doing this ourselves. In fact, no one but us *can* decide."

THE NEXT morning, Dan called Paul twice, expressing more doubts and reservations. I went over to the nursing home, and Paul and I spent the afternoon talking. Paul made an impassioned plea for love.

"These little questions of Dan's are just the beginning of the nay-saying," he said. "But we have to walk through this storm united."

I looked at him doubtfully.

"What about the intensity of our feelings? What about the miraculous aspect of all this, our finding each other so late, and in such an unlikely place? Are we going to allow that to be clouded over by 'what about this' and 'what about that'?"

I listened and agreed with what he said, but my stomach was churning.

"If I have to say goodbye to you, I don't know what could possibly take your place," Paul said earnestly. "There is no one like you."

"I feel the same way about you, Paul," I said. "It's not that I don't like my life. It's just that there's something missing. I guess that's why I'm here."

"It seems to me," Paul said, "that life comes in a series of twenty years, or at least it has for me. The first twenty years, you don't know your butt from a hole in the ground. The second twenty, life is good, you're going for a ride. Whee! Isn't this fun? The third twenty, the road starts to get bumpy. You have some rough rides. You don't know where the hell you are anymore or whether you're going in the right direction."

"I've just gotten on the rocky road," I said. "Tell me what's ahead."

"That's just it. Nobody knows. You've got to get used to the mystery. It's all right not to know."

"Just the thought of living together fills me with fear, Paul," I said. "I'm worried about your health and your memory loss, too."

"I've noticed how you watch and comment on that. I'm amused by my memory. Humor is the best way to handle it."

"Yes, but it scares me. What if you left the stove on and started a fire?"

"I've never once done anything dangerous like that!" Paul said, defensively. "You have no reason to put me in that category! Others have voiced that concern. After Lila died and we were all in turmoil about where I was going, Lila's nephew raised the point about my being dangerous to myself and to the house. His wife said, 'Brad! I can't believe you said that!' Which I mention just to show how they lined up on the issue. See? I remembered that, didn't I?"

"That's not fair, Paul," I said, wounded.

"I'm just bringing it up as a point of contention," Paul said more evenly. "I have always prided myself on being safety conscious. Whenever someone would leave grocery bags or bread wrappers on the stove, I would go around and pick them up. It's old people who are *more* vigilant, because they're concerned about being labeled and categorized as forgetful and senile!"

"Do you remember what daily life outside the nursing home is like?" I asked, changing the subject. "Cooking and cleaning and shopping and doing the laundry. Getting the car fixed, calling a plumber, finding someone to haul away the dead tree limbs in the front yard. Do you really want all that responsibility again?"

Paul smiled. "Yes, I remember, and I want it back. I've seen myself in your kitchen, making dinner and feeding the cats while you're working. I want it for all its ordinariness."

The talking calmed me down. That and lying on Paul's chest, listening to his heart beat.

THE NEXT day at work, I was again stricken with periods of anxiety. What was becoming of my life? My cherished, career-oriented life? How could I possibly be considering so drastic a change? Paul needed

135

care now and would need even more later. Everything would shift in his direction. But I wanted *me* to be at the center of my life. Was I being selfish? If I really loved Paul, wouldn't I *want* to take care of him? If I didn't, what did that say about me?

I called Paul that evening around eight.

"What?" Paul said when he heard I was still in the office. "It's not safe to be downtown after hours. We've got problems, but they're not that bad!"

"I'm sorry I was so moody yesterday," I said. "But I've got a lot of scary things on my mind."

"Dan called again today. He said, 'Have you seen her since Saturday?' And I said, 'Yes, she was here half the day yesterday.' That seemed to appease him a little bit."

"I've felt anxious all day, Paul. Things are moving too fast."

"I don't want to make you anxious, honey. I want to be the best friend you ever had."

"And I want the same for you," I said.

"I had a moment of enlightenment today," Paul said. "I realized that maybe I was putting too much pressure on you, with my desires and my intensity."

"Yes," I said. "You are a passionate man, and I am a careful, deliberate woman. I'm afraid I'll get *swept away* by your intensity and, later, *overwhelmed* by it."

"I've been thinking of an alternate plan," Paul said. "A way for us to be together on a part-time basis."

"I'm listening," I said.

"I know how important your career is. You've worked hard for that, and I don't want to interfere. I'd rather jump off a bridge."

I laughed. "That's a bit melodramatic, don't you think?"

"Part of me wants you all to myself," Paul continued. "But another part says, 'Go, learn, work, earn! The world is yours, my darling!'"

"Thank you for that, Paul. I love both parts of you, but this conversation has helped me choose between them. I've decided that I want the world, and I want our relationship to stay the way it is. Will that be enough for you?"

"Oh, honey, I love what we have now. I wouldn't want to do anything to jeopardize it. It's already more than I ever thought we could have. The other, living together, was my wildest dream. I knew it probably wouldn't happen, but I had to give it a shot."

"I had that dream myself for a little while," I said. "But to be honest, it's more than I can handle."

"Let's forget it, then," Paul said.

And so we did.

II EMPTY ROOMS

Paul had come to accept his chronic conditions, but sometimes the smaller problems really got him down: an irritated eye, a throbbing knee, a pain in his kidney, a stiff neck that lasted for days. One time he had a violent reaction to something he had eaten for lunch.

"I feel bad," Paul said over the phone. "Why don't you come over and rub my stomach?"

"I would, Paul, but I've got a presentation due in the morning. I'm going to be up half the night now. You'll be OK."

"I might be dead in the morning," Paul said morosely.

"I'll call first thing tomorrow to check on you," I said.

When he hung up, Paul felt sad and lonely. He spent the night in his chair, shuffling back and forth to the bathroom. He dwelt on the cramps in his stomach, the nausea, the diarrhea. He obsessed about our relationship and me, and that led him down a darker path. Could this be the beginning of the end? Perhaps stomach cancer? A fast-growing tumor?

"For a few hours, I truly thought I might die," Paul reported the next morning. "But I should have known they wouldn't come after me over a little thing like an upset stomach."

Around that time, a new guy moved on to Paul's wing. He and his wife walked into the dining room one afternoon and introduced themselves.

"This is Joe Reynolds," the woman said. "He's just moved in. I'm Thelma Reynolds."

From a distance, Mr. Reynolds appeared to be bald. When he got closer, though, you could see that he had a thin layer of fuzzy white hair over his pink head. He was tall, with a potbelly, and he squinted through very thick eye glasses. Mrs. Reynolds was a compact woman with curly brown hair. She had the leathery look of someone who had spent a lot of time outdoors.

We invited them to join Paul's table.

"Are you his daughter?" Thelma asked politely.

"No, I'm his friend," I replied.

"Joe's blind," Thelma said. "I'm here to feed him. He could do it on his own, but he spills it all over and gets frustrated."

"It's nice that you can be here for his first day," I said.

"Yes," Thelma said. "He doesn't know anybody yet."

Joe's opening line in the conversation was a sports question. He asked Paul what he thought about a baseball player who had recently been in the news.

"Who's that?" Paul asked. "I don't know anything about him."

"He's a coach," Joe said. "They've asked him to resign."

"Is that so?" said Paul. "I guess I did hear something about him on the news. I like sports, but I never followed it much on TV."

"He's still got a good head of hair," Joe said to his wife, referring to Paul. "He's a handsome man."

"Why, sir!" Paul said, feigning embarrassment.

Thelma launched into a private conversation with Paul, but she wasn't used to his low voice. Pretty soon, she was directing her questions to me.

"How long has he been here?" she asked.

"Long enough to know better," Paul said.

"You're going to have trouble getting a straight answer out of him," I told Thelma.

"Likes to joke, eh?" Joe said. "That's OK. I like to joke myself."

"The man across from you is Morris," I said. "But he's not being very talkative today."

"Oh, yes, I already know Morris," Joe said. "We're roommates."

Thelma looked at Morris and asked me, "Can you understand him?"

"Sometimes," I said.

Thelma made small talk about the food, which apparently was much better than the food at Joe's previous nursing home.

"That place, everything was mush," Thelma said. "And they didn't watch people. Twice he got out and wandered around the grounds. He was wandering then, which is why we put him in there. The police found him in the park."

I touched Joe's arm to get his attention. "That must have been frightening," I said. "Do you remember that incident?"

"Oh, yes," he said.

"We pulled him out of there," Thelma continued. "So far, this place seems much better."

As Thelma fed Joe, she provided a running commentary: "The soup is chicken noodle. Do you want to try some? You like chicken noodle."

"What's this?" Joe said, feeling his way around the sandwich on his plate.

"Grilled cheese," Thelma said.

Joe picked it up and began eating tentatively.

"How old are you?" Thelma asked Paul.

"Let's see, how old am I?" Paul mused. "I'm eighty-four."

"You're doing pretty good for eighty-four," Thelma said. She looked at Joe. "He's ninety-seven."

"No kidding!" I said, surprised.

Thelma watched as Paul pulled gingerly on a sandwich with his teeth.

"You're not eating much," she commented.

"My teeth hurt," Paul explained. "New dentures."

"I know how that feels," Thelma said. "I had all my teeth pulled when I was in my fifties. Every tooth in my mouth is false."

When we finished eating, we all walked down the hall together. A large green fish made of felt and stuffed with cotton batting was now hanging outside Joe and Morris's door.

"That's how Joe finds his room," Thelma explained. "He used to love fishing."

A couple of weeks later, Paul was describing the day's lunch over the phone.

"It was like a morgue in there for the first half of the meal," he reported. "I just said a few things to get their minds working and to remind people that we can still communicate. An aide came over to help your friend—ninety-seven—who was doing his usual routine: 'Tell me what's on my plate. What the hell is this stuff? Is anyone going to help me get some food around here?' Then he started baiting me. 'He's got the best lookin' woman in the place! Boy, is she a looker!' They all got involved after that. What's his name's wife . . ."

"You mean Morris's wife, Bea, was there?" I asked.

"Yes, and she thought she had to protect my interests. She informed them all that you were getting a good deal, too. 'They've got each *other*,' she said. Ninety-seven reported that he'd talked to you and held your hand and found you exceedingly nice. He was tossing these comments out like horseshoes. Everyone was laughing, and for all sorts of reasons. Dirty reasons, romantic reasons, and for the pure pleasure of the talk."

"And what were you doing?" I asked.

"I was grinning the whole length of the conversation," Paul said. "When I left, I turned and said, 'That was very good entertainment. You make sure you all come back tomorrow, because there will be something even more spectacular.' They all broke up over that because they knew you were coming to visit tonight."

PAUL AND I were on the phone again.

"I'm going down in my chair now," Paul said. "I'm halfway down. When I stop talking, I'll have dropped into place."

I heard a few beeps and the dial tone.

"Hello? Hello?" I said into an empty receiver. I hung up, fed the cats, and called him back. Paul answered on the first ring.

"That was an abrupt way to cut a person off," I said.

"I wouldn't cut you off if the king demanded it, honey."

"What happened? It sounded like you hit a button."

"I pressed a whole face panel. I accidentally sat on the phone."

"Are you all right? You had such a bad day yesterday, I was worried."

"I knew you were," Paul said. "You thought I was going to go after you left, didn't you?"

"Well, no, I didn't exactly think that, but I guess it's always a possibility."

"Yes, it is," Paul said. "Optimistic, aren't we?"

"RE-alistic," I said.

"That's right, honey. We've got to face the music."

THE GREEN fish didn't do much to anchor Joe Reynolds. He had started wandering again. Paul described Joe as "slightly off center, like a crankshaft."

"Poor guy," Paul said. "I saw him walking up and down the hall last night around midnight. He's lonely. It's pathetic, really. He wants what I've got."

"Doesn't his wife come around?" I asked.

"I haven't seen her since that first day," Paul said. "It's always one of his two daughters."

"That's too bad. Shall I go over to his room and cheer him up?" I said, teasing.

"Don't you *dare*," Paul said. "Seriously, I wouldn't take a chance on his behavior. He's always wandering into the women's rooms. Well, on his behalf, they're the only rooms on this wing except for mine. But Eleanor said if he comes fumbling around her room one more time, she'll get a gun and shoot him."

Later that week, Paul and I were propped on his bed, watching the seven o'clock news. We heard a rattling of the handle, and the door opened. Joe walked in, looking confused. He was wearing striped pajamas.

"Is this my room?" Joe said.

"No," said Paul. "You're down the hall."

Joe turned and moved toward the first door on his left.

"That's the bathroom, Joe," Paul said.

"Then where the hell is . . . ?"

"I'd better get him before he wets his pants," Paul said to me. He gradually inched himself off the bed and took a few halting steps toward Joe, taking his arm and pulling him gently toward the door. Paul pointed down the hall.

"Right there, the one with the big green fish. Remember?"

"Oh, yeah," Joe said. "Thanks. Thank you very much."

"Truth be known," Paul said, returning to the bed. "He's trying to steal my girl."

Joe was gone within a month, transferred to the third-floor dementia wing. He had been grabbing at the aides, and his confusion had worsened. One night, late, he'd come into Paul's room, where Paul was sleeping in his chair. An aide followed him in and caught him by the arm.

"What are you doing in here?" she said gruffly. "This is Mr. Paul's room."

Joe shrugged her off. "Now, see here," he said. "This gentleman is my *friend*!"

Softening a little, the aide said, "Well, it's one o'clock in the morning. These are not visiting hours."

Paul and I visited Joe on a Sunday afternoon, a few days after he had moved. We found him napping on his bed in a darkened room. We paused at the foot of the bed, wondering whether we should wake him.

"Joe," Paul said, trying to increase the volume in his voice. "Joe." He shook the foot of the bed.

"Hello, Joe," I said.

"Yes? Who is it?" Joe mumbled.

"It's Paul and Ruth," Paul said. "We came to see how you're doing up here." Paul extended his hand. Joe reached into the air and shook it.

"Not too good," Joe said. "I need a shave. Can anyone give me a shave?"

"They'll be around," Paul said. "Ask an aide, and she'll take care of you."

"How do you like your new room?" I asked.

Lying on his side, Joe shrugged.

"We won't keep you from your nap," Paul said. "We'll come around another time." We had been there less than five minutes, but Paul was ready to leave.

In the elevator, I said, "Joe's room is rather spartan, don't you think?"

"There's nothing more depressing than an old man in an empty room," Paul said solemnly.

After that visit, I came across a poem in a collection of literary works about aging and old age. The Iraqi poet Buland al-Haydari, a man of Paul's generation, spent years in political exile and often wrote of loneliness and longing. His poem "Old Age" captures some of what Paul already knew about Joe and the emotional state of many old men:

Another winter,
And here am I,
By the side of the stove,
Dreaming that a woman might dream of me,

That I might bury in her breast
A secret she would not mock;
Dreaming that in my fading years
I might spring forth as light,
And she would say:
>This light is mine;
>Let no woman draw near it.
Here by the side of the stove,
Another winter,
And here am I,
Spinning my dreams and fearing them.
Afraid her eyes would mock
My bald, idiotic head,
My graying, aged soul,
>Afraid her feet would kick
>My love.
>And here, by the side of the stove,
>I would be lightly mocked by woman.
Alone,
Without love, or dreams, or a woman,
And tomorrow I shall die of the cold within,
Here, by the side of the stove.[1]

PAUL AND I spent Christmas Eve 1997 at my house. On Christmas Day, I made breakfast while Paul lay in bed and stroked the cat. I brought him his pills and a glass of water with a straw. From a reclining position, Paul kissed me good morning and made a playful grab for me. I eluded his grasp and returned to the kitchen to stir the oatmeal. I set the table and placed a gift-wrapped box on Paul's chair.

"What have you done?" Paul said, entering the kitchen in one of my bathrobes. He had chosen the plaid flannel over the pink chenille. "Oh, honey, it's too much. I can't take it."

"Don't be ridiculous," I said. "You don't even know what it is."

Paul struggled to unwrap the package. Finally, he tore off the paper and opened the box. He removed a cream-colored cardigan.

"Darling, it's a beauty. But it's too much."

"I'm insulted!" I said in mock offense. "This is a sign of my love and appreciation."

"You spent too much," Paul said, shaking his head.

"It's just a cotton sweater, ordered from a catalog."

"This sweater is good news to me," Paul said. "So many times I go down to the dinner table and wish I had a wrap to put over my shoulders. Something like a sweater can make all the difference in a day."

While I finished making breakfast, Paul spread the newspaper on the table and skimmed the headlines. I set a plate of toast and eggs in front of him and began to read the paper myself. Sun streamed through the kitchen, and the room smelled of coffee.

I looked up and saw that Paul wasn't eating. His eyes had a glazed look and his right arm lay in his plate. Without saying a word, he picked up the jelly jar and brought it to his lips.

"Paul? Paul? What's wrong?" I asked. He was breathing fast through his nose. His face had gone gray. He made a movement as if to rest his head on his arms.

"Paul!" I leapt out of my chair and moved in behind him. "Paul, can you hear me?"

He made no sound, other than the heavy breathing. Then, very slowly and deliberately, he rose and steadied himself, holding onto the edge of the table.

"Do you want to lie down?" I asked.

Paul's face was waxy and lifeless. His eyes were cast downward, but he didn't seem to be looking at anything. He turned from the table. I grabbed his waist. His skinny body was stiff and heavy. I pushed him around the corner into the bedroom, where he slumped onto the bed. "Bathroom," he said, finally. "I have to go before I lie down." His voice was a thin whisper.

I helped Paul back through the kitchen and down the hall to the bathroom. He slowly pulled aside the robe and lowered himself onto the toilet seat in tiny increments. "It's a long way down," he joked wearily. I left him there for several minutes, checking in periodically. "Are you all right? Do you need help?"

I was sitting at the kitchen table when he finally emerged.

"You scared me," I said.

"I scared myself," Paul replied.

"What happened?"

"I felt faint. I could hear you, but I couldn't talk to you. It was like there were two of us pulling, you from your side and me from mine. You kept saying, 'Paul,' and I kept saying to myself, 'Don't go to sleep. Not here, not now.' I had to fight my way back."

THIS "GOING away" happened again a couple months later when I was out of town at a conference.

"I had that same dizzy, distant feeling," Paul said. "The nurse was calling my name, but I was far away. Then I thought about you, and I came back. I didn't want to go without saying goodbye."

"I'm so glad you didn't!" I said.

"When you're away, I mean really gone, I feel myself losing ground. Then you come home, and with the first touch of your hand, I feel myself coming back. Does that sound crazy?"

"Not at all," I said, "It makes perfect sense."

"I knew you'd understand," Paul said. "Love is a powerful thing. I don't even have the words to describe it. But there's a power in it that makes me want to live forever."

Another time when I was out of town, Paul fell in his room and couldn't get up. It wasn't the actual fall that worried him, but the way the staff reacted to it. Paul wouldn't even say the word "fall" when he reported the incident to me.

"It wasn't a fall," he insisted. "I slid down the side of my chair. Then there wasn't anything I could grab hold of to get back up. I felt myself losing my balance, and I reached back for the seat of the chair, and I caught hold of that soft blanket instead. I knew I was headed for the floor, and I wanted something cozy to snuggle up to when I got there. I teetered and slid, landing on my side, facing the wall."

"You weren't hurt, were you?" I asked.

"Not a scratch," Paul said. "This is not a big deal, although the staff is trying to make it one. It can't be a fall, because a fall suggests hurtling through the air, and I didn't do that. I lost my balance, that's all."

"OK, so you slid down the side of the chair and lay on your side with the blanket," I said, trying to get the facts straight. "How'd you get back up again?"

"I called and called for an aide, but they're never around when you need one, and they're always there when you don't. Anyway, I must have lain in that spot for an hour. It was around five in the morning. Finally, someone came in and helped me up. Then she told the nurse, who called Dan. Can you imagine? Bothering him at that time of the morning? She got him out of bed to tell him she had to file an incident report."

I knew that falling in a nursing home was bad news. "Number of falls" is a common indicator of health status. An increase in falls means a decline in health.

"But I don't call it a fall," Paul repeated. "I haven't fallen in the three and a half years I've been here, although that's one reason the doctor thought I should be living in a nursing home. When I went to lunch today, everybody was avoiding my eyes, like something awful had happened, and they didn't want to talk about it. I said out loud, to anyone who was listening, 'I DIDN'T FALL! I SLID DOWN THE SIDE OF MY CHAIR!' Finally, one of the ladies at the table behind me said, cautiously, 'Are you all right now, Paul?'"

AROUND EASTER of that year, a month or so after the "slide," Paul had another unusual experience. He had gone to sleep, and he woke up needing to use the bathroom. When he returned to bed, he was surprised to find it occupied. Lila's sister, Ruby, was stretched out and snoring lightly. An overnight case filled with women's things lay open on the floor. Paul turned to his chair, and there was Lila, with curlers in her hair, sound asleep. She was wearing stylish new glasses that made her look prettier and younger than he had ever seen her. An afghan was partially draped over her legs. Paul pulled it down to cover her bare feet. Another woman, younger, stood silently in the corner. Paul didn't know who she was. He opened the door and walked out into the bright hallway.

"Mr. Mason, what are you doing up at this hour?" the nurse said.

"I don't know," Paul said absently. "I must have had a dream. There's no place—I need to go back and check my room." He returned to find everything back to normal.

After that, Paul's health declined steadily. He got pneumonia, was admitted to the hospital, and came back to the nursing home in a state of exhaustion. He lay in bed most of the time, barely able to reach for the phone.

One Sunday afternoon, I sat on the edge of his bed, chatting about this and that, trying to keep his mind occupied. A Detroit Tigers game was on TV.

"Did you feel that?" Paul said, suddenly.

"What? I didn't feel anything."

"Vibrations."

"Where?" I asked.

"Inside and out, all around me. Waves of vibrations."

"How does it feel?" I said, concerned.

"Good. Very pleasurable. I wish you could feel it."

Now Paul was not just thin, he was gaunt. I brought him one of his favorite foods, strawberry shortcake with real whipped cream, to try and stimulate his appetite. As I was feeding him tiny bites, one of the nurses walked in and said, "Oh, no! We can't have that! He might aspirate!" She took away the shortcake and handed Paul a Styrofoam cup filled with a clear, viscous substance.

"I can't stand this stuff," Paul complained. "It's all I ever get anymore, and it tastes awful." It was something the aides called prowater, but Paul called it "heavy water." It was supposed to keep him hydrated and provide nourishment, but it took all the remaining pleasure out of eating. Most of the time, Paul refused to drink it.

IT WAS an unseasonably warm day in May when Paul died. He had been hospitalized again and had now stopped eating completely. He had declined the feeding tube, despite Dan's pleas and counterarguments. "Damn salesman," Paul grumbled. "But I'm proud of him." Paul didn't want to go before his time, but he didn't want to stick around too long and be a burden, either. "I've never died before," he apologized. "I'm not sure how to go about it. Please forgive me if I make mistakes."

On the evening of my last visit, Paul was sleeping when I entered the hospital room. I moved to the side of the bed and stood there quietly. His body looked very old and frail. Someone had removed his dentures, which hollowed out his cheeks. He lay slightly askew on the pillow. His right arm, badly bruised from the IVs, rested on top of the sheet. The left one, also bruised, lay under the covers. I looked at the tissue paper skin, the twitching right forefinger, the sharp points of breastbone. When I touched his arm, he gave a raspy cough.

"Hmm?" Paul said, opening his eyes.

"Hello, Mr. Mason," I said, smiling.

"Hello, Mrs. Mason."

I leaned down to kiss his cheek.

"Don't kiss me too much," Paul said. "I must look terrible."

I kissed him lightly on the lips.

"Thank you, darlin'." Paul managed a smile. "I'm so tired."

"Go right ahead and sleep," I said. "I'll just sit next to you in the chair."

After a while, Paul opened his eyes and scanned the air in front of him. "Who's that woman sitting there?" he said, looking at an empty chair in the corner. He began mumbling to himself. He talked off and on for nearly an hour, describing the scenes passing before him. Occasionally, he raised his right arm in a come hither motion, beckoning to someone I couldn't see. I leaned closer to hear. He was talking to Lila.

"Please, do something, Lila. Please!" He became increasingly agitated.

"Let's go! Come on, let's go! Turn the corner fast! All right? All right?"

"All right, Paul," I said, watching him closely.

"Take the two short ones, quick, before they come. Do you have them?" he asked urgently.

"Yes, I have them," I said.

"They're coming!"

Paul returned to his whispering, punctuated by brief outbursts.

"Damn!" he said once. And then, more calmly, "It's moving faster now."

I leaned forward and kissed his face, trying to bring him back. He didn't move, but he said, "I love you."

"I love you, too," I said, beginning to cry.

A nurse came to the door. "Mr. Mason?"

"Yes," he said, softly.

"I'm going to have to take some more blood," she said. She flipped on the overhead lights, flooding the room with a garish white.

"I can't believe you're still taking blood!" I said irritably.

"This is the last time, I think. The doctor requested it."

It took her a while to find a vein. She drew a little blood from the right arm, but it wasn't enough. "They'll probably send it back," she said, shaking her head. She asked Paul to make a fist. When he complied, she punctured his hand.

The nurse made no conversation with either one of us. When she had finished the task, she gathered up the vials and left the room, hitting the light switch on her way out.

"At least she had sense enough to turn out the light," I growled.

"She's just doing her job," Paul said.

He raised his right hand and touched his chin and then his nose, as if to see whether his body was still there. Then he beckoned, calling someone forward. For reasons I didn't understand, I found these gestures comforting. It seemed that Paul was receiving assistance of some kind. A few weeks later, I read Elisabeth Kubler-Ross's memoir *The Wheel of Life*, in which she describes her work on death and dying. She explains how, as they near death, many patients have "extremely vivid experiences" while conversing with people in the room that others can't see. Based on years of research and observation, Kubler-Ross concludes that "no one dies alone."

It was nearly dark outside now. The room was dimly lit from the parking lot below.

Paul fell silent, and I rose from the chair. "I'm going home now," I said, touching his arm.

Paul opened his eyes. "I'm going home, too."

"I know," I said, tears in my eyes. I kissed him goodbye.

The phone rang at seven the next morning. It was Dan, calling to say that Paul had died in the middle of the night.

THE FUNERAL was held the following Saturday in Brighton, a distant suburb of Detroit, where Paul had once owned a feed and garden store. Early that morning, I went to the farmer's market and bought every wildflower available, fashioning a riotous bouquet. It was an eccentric contribution to the more somber arrangements at the funeral home, but it seemed in keeping with Paul's personality. After the service, Dan offered me one of the arrangements, and I chose the wild flowers, now slightly wilted, but still full of color. I delivered them that evening to the nurses' station on Paul's floor.

Paul's recliner and all his possessions had already been moved, and someone else occupied Room 201. A woman sat in a chair watching TV.

I walked into Morris's room. It was early evening and Morris was tucked in for the night. His hospital bed looked like a crib. The rails were up, and they were covered with bumper pads. I stood at the side of the bed and called his name softly. Morris's bulging eyes opened immediately.

"Hello, Morris," I said. "I've come to say goodbye. Paul's funeral was this afternoon."

Morris reached up and took my hand with his two rigid ones. He whispered something inaudible.

"You were a good friend to Paul, and he appreciated it," I said.

Morris continued to whisper, not words, but a mumbling stream of sound. Still, I understood that he was consoling me.

"You were a friend to me, too, Morris, and I thank you for it," I said.

Morris pulled me close and gave me something resembling a kiss on the cheek, although he couldn't pucker his lips. I told him about the funeral and that I had left some flowers at the nurses' station.

"They are a tribute to spring and to new beginnings," I said. "When you wheel by on your way to breakfast, say a little prayer of thanks for our time with Paul, won't you?"

I had thought about putting together a scrapbook of photos and a few of Paul's stories so the staff and residents would have something to remember him by, but I just didn't have the energy for it. It would have included these words, which Paul once left on my answering machine:

I just called to see if you're loving anybody today. If you're not loving somebody, you're wasting your time. These are my words of wisdom, from this side of eighty.

12 ETHICS OF CARE

I have just told you an unusual love story. My hope is that it will become an "evocative narrative" in your thinking about age. The communications scholars Art Bochner and Janet Rushing describe such narratives, in contrast to conventional academic reports, as stories that "long to be used rather than analyzed; to be told and retold rather than theorized and settled; to offer lessons for further conversation rather than undebatable conclusions; and to substitute the companionship of intimate detail for the loneliness of abstracted facts." Another narrative researcher, the rhetorician Wayne Booth, claims that fiction, autobiography, memoir, and even some journalistic accounts can teach us "essential ethical truths about the world of health, disease, medicine, and the right and wrong ways of facing death." How do narratives work in this way? By showing us, not only how to *think* about ethical issues but also how it *feels* to struggle with them. Narratives broaden our understanding *and* our sensibilities. In experiencing the emotional power of a narrative, readers may be forced to think harder about issues in their own lives. This is what the psychiatrist Robert Coles refers to as the moral "call of stories." The cultural historian Thomas R. Cole goes even further in describing some stories as "vehicles of cultural meaning and individual soul making."[1]

I invite readers to step back from the love story now and consider its larger social meanings beyond the personal. For me, the story raises many questions about how we relate to others, especially those who are different from us in terms of age, gender, and able-bodiedness. In this chapter, I draw on the academic literature in feminist studies and gerontology to address several questions that interest me as a woman trying to understand my relationship with Paul, as well as a gerontologist trying to understand the meanings of "quality care" and "quality of life" in old age:

What is the connection between love and care?

What are the characteristics of caring people, and how do they behave toward one another?

How can caring relationships enhance personal growth and social change?

How might we create more caring environments in which we can grow old and die with integrity?

Love and Care

The kind of love I have described in this memoir goes beyond the infatuation we usually see depicted in magazines, movies, and romance novels. These are patriarchal constructions that, as bell hooks notes in her feminist analysis of love, focus on games playing and manipulations, competition and power, dominance and submission. Hooks's feminist construction of love emphasizes honesty and truth-telling, with the purpose of creating a transformational force that nurtures the spiritual and emotional development of both partners.[2] In such loving relationships, mutual growth, rather than sexual attraction, is the binding principle, although sexual attraction may exist, too. When it does, sex will help foster growth.

Paul and I both experienced our relationship as generative and healing on many levels. In his presence, I felt unconditionally loved, accepted, and supported, and I tried to do the same for him. I knew that Paul wanted what was best for me, even when it conflicted with what he wanted for himself. He was careful not to stand in the way of my development as a person or a professional and, in fact, reveled in the changes he saw in me. He said to me once, "You're becoming more uniquely you all the time, and it's a pleasure to see." For a man to feel, express, and act on an attitude of total acceptance toward the woman he loves requires a great deal of self-esteem, maturity, and courage. It also requires faith—in one's self, in the other, and in the transformative potential of love, even when we can't predict or control it. As theologian Thomas Moore explains, "unconditional love means that we don't love on the condition that we understand."[3] Transformative love is what emotionally healthy women want with their partners, yet they rarely experience it in their relationships with men.

Hooks explains why. The male in patriarchal societies is conditioned to feel threatened by the power and potential in the female, and he acts accordingly, limiting and undermining her in ways that even he does not understand. The woman, who has also internalized the conditioning of patriarchy, feels threatened by her *own* potential and subconsciously limits herself. Hooks urges us to do the hard emotional work necessary to overcome this social conditioning and develop mutually empowering ways of relating. A first step is to recognize and challenge the patriarchal imaginary in which narratives of power always trump narratives of love. In the power narrative, sex (as a form of domination) is privileged over love (as a form of mutual caregiving), and love is relegated to the private domain of women.

Drawing on Diane Ackerman's *A Natural History of Love*, hooks traces the cultural shift in America away from mutual care in heterosexual relationships. Earlier ideas about love that "emphasized a soul mate, reciprocal care and devotion were supplanted by an emphasis on sacrificial care and nurturance, [and] love became solely woman's work." Over time, women have become complicit in this undertaking by acting as if men *can't* be expected to care and nurture in equal measure, and by assuming a position of superiority over men in the emotional realm. Hooks argues that for personal and social change to occur in love relationships, both men and women must stop "clinging to the rewards and forms of power [that] patriarchy extends to them for *not* being loving"[4]

What hooks says about individuals in love relationships is true for people in all caring relationships, including family caregivers and those who are dependent on them, doctors and patients, nursing aides and nursing home residents. In all cases, the best caregiving will occur in relationships that are built on mutual regard and support for the development of each other's highest self. This, in fact, is the concept of care that is promoted by feminist philosophers who study the ethics of care, as well as by researchers and practitioners who see the spiritual potential in caring relationships.

Many feminists define "care" as both a value and a practice, a way of thinking and behaving in relationships. "To care" is to consider the well-being of others in relation to one's own well-being. From a feminist perspective, all human beings are relational and interdependent, not autonomous and independent, and relationships are essential to human identity. Therefore, understanding "care" requires an understanding of how family, culture, and history affect our decisions about caring. As moral agents, we are each "encumbered selves," whose decisions rely on and impact a great many others. Even "autonomy" and "independence" can be understood relationally: "That we can think and act as if we were independent depends on a network of social relations making it possible for us to do so."[5] In a feminist ethics of care, the needs and rights of caregivers are as important as the needs and rights of those for whom they provide care. The goal of moral decision-making, then, is to foster social bonds and cooperation so that we might discover what is most beneficial for each participant in a caring relationship. The philosopher Virginia Held lists the following principles of a feminist ethics of care:

Acknowledging and meeting the needs of others is "morally salient." We are all, male and female alike, morally responsible for helping other human beings to live and prosper. Helping relations occur in both the private and public realms, in the family and society, in institutions, economies, and the environment.

Decisions about care are best made in the context of specific relationships. In fact, the particulars of relationships often take priority over adherence to abstract principles, including the patriarchal principle that all women are "natural" caregivers who should willingly sacrifice themselves for the benefit of others.

Care necessarily engages the emotions, negative and positive, including anger, fear and resentment, as well as compassion, sympathy and empathy. Decisions about care that are based entirely on reason are reductionist and deficient.

For feminists, caring attitudes, such as attentiveness, sensitivity, and responsiveness to others' needs, are intertwined with caring practices. "Care," then, is a way of *behaving* that "builds trust and mutual concern and connectedness between persons, not through individual actions, but as a continual practice that develops over time, along with caring attitudes." An important caring behavior is the promotion of "mutual autonomy," which Held defines as "mutual understandings and acceptances of how much sharing of time, space, daily decisions, and so on there will be, and how much independently arrived at activity," thus limiting the potential for "overbearing attention" and "benevolent smothering."[6] Such caring practices are "transformative" in the sense that they assist everyone involved in becoming "morally admirable" in Held's worldview and "self-actualized" in hooks's worldview.

There is often a narrative component to a feminist ethics of care. The philosopher Margaret Urban Walker includes "narrative appreciation" as one of four main principles in her philosophy of care. She argues that people in caring relationships are obliged to understand each other's stories—"the telling details of their lives and the meanings and consequences they ascribe to them." Says Walker, the "intertwining of selves and stories in narrative constructions which locate what is at stake, what is needed, and what is possible is at the heart of moral thinking for many women and feminist writers." Similarly, philosopher Robin Fiore argues that care involves knowing one another fully and acknowledging each other's complexity. She uses the term "due recognition" to describe this knowing. It involves "responding to others on the basis of their self-conceptions [and] attending to those features of their lives that they regard as identity constituting, rather than treating them according to [our] own favored way of seeing them."[7] For these reasons, feminist ethics are sometimes called "discursive ethics," emphasizing the importance of negotiating difference in caring relationships. Following feminist ethics, "we are to listen to [others'] stories and attempt to negotiate with them to arrive, if at all possible, at a course that all affected parties find acceptable."[8] The chapter in my story called "Care Conference" is meant to suggest the relational and discursive process that Paul, his family, and I went through in deciding whether he would remain in the nursing home. Knowing another's life stories, along with the meanings ascribed to them, is sometimes all we have when an elder is not able to communicate his needs and desires. Fortunately, Paul was more than able to speak for himself and to engage in mutual decision-making. For my part, I had to listen carefully, assess my own needs and abilities, state my position clearly, and honor my feelings. The "Care Conference" chapter characterizes everyone involved as caring people who want only the best for each other—

which is how I saw things then and still do—even though neither Dan's family nor I was prepared to care for Paul at home.

Characteristics of Caring People

As should be clear from the discussion so far, the caring person will have the intention to care, as well as the disposition and capabilities to care, and will engage in caring practices that are appropriate to specific relationships. If a person has a caring motive but does not engage in the work of care, that person *wants* to care but is not yet caring. Held's distinction between "charity" and "care" helps show the difference between a virtuous person (one who *believes* in doing good) and a caring person (one who *does* good). Charity is based on a virtuous motive but not a mutually caring relationship; care requires a virtuous motive, followed through with caring practices in a caring relationship. As Held notes, care is always preferable to charity because it allows for expressions of identity and agency on the part of the other. Care involves trust and mutuality; charity involves "benevolent domination" and is often not what the other needs, wants, or deserves. Through the interdependent relationships of care, as opposed to the dependent relationships of charity, differences in power will be negotiated, and the vulnerable will more likely be empowered, rather than disempowered.[9]

Caring people demonstrate various kinds of intelligence, including interpersonal intelligence that involves sensitivity to and respect for others' feelings; an ability to assess the kinds of care needed in a given situation; and an ability to engage in caring practices that are appropriate for the situation. Caring people consciously reflect on the practices of care and know their value, and they also know how to care for themselves. They will engage in different caring practices, depending on the relationship, and they will disengage from entangling relationships that impede their agency and ability to care. Held makes these qualities clear in the following examples: A working daughter whose elderly parents are adequately cared for and who are caring people themselves can show that she is a caring person with an occasional phone call that affirms the commitment and bond between them. This same daughter must engage in more demanding practices of care with her three-year-old child. She is still a caring person to her child in daycare if the child feels continually loved and has a close relationship with her parents. If the daughter finds herself in a relationship that demands more of her than she has to give or that involves what Walker calls a "plague of commitments," because she is a person who cares for herself and her continued ability to care for others, she will change or leave that relationship. Such overwhelming relationships are very common in the lives of women, who, products of patriarchal conditioning, often assume too much of men's responsibility for caring and fail to care adequately for themselves. Additionally, because it does not value care as much as it values power, patriarchal society does not provide the cultural and economic support needed to develop caring networks that would ease the burden of care for men and women alike.[10]

Potential for Growth in Caring Relationships

In *Counting on Kindness*, the social worker Wendy Lustbader claims that there are rich possibilities for "revival" and "renewal" in the experiences of illness, dependency, and dying both for caregivers and for those receiving care, but only if we initiate a "reconstruction of our internal world." This "reconstruction" entails the acceptance of change and the ability to let go of the past and embrace the future, however uncertain. It also requires that we overcome our self-centeredness, that we enter willingly into new relationships of caring, and that we learn to assert our own needs in order to maintain personal integrity. Most important is that we learn to grant illness, disability, and old age "their own validity." To do so, we must challenge the American ethos of independence as the only form of strength and the belief that *doing* is better than *being*, both evidence of a culture that privileges power over love. Lustbader suggests that we introduce phrases into our vocabulary that will reorient our thinking, such as "successful frailty" and "turning the insults of illness into privileges of being." These rephrasings suggest what Thomas R. Cole calls the "moral contours of dependence." He argues that dependence carries its own moral challenges and responsibilities, among which are learning to accept help graciously, reciprocating care in whatever ways we can, and preparing for our own death. Cole draws attention to the paradox of decline and spirituality: although patriarchal society teaches that decline represents a loss of personal power that should be denigrated, spiritual traditions teach that bodily decline often leads to psychic growth, which should be celebrated. From a moral standpoint, those involved in caregiving relationships should therefore attend to the needs of the spirit as well as the body.[11]

I find that Lustbader's ethic of care aligns perfectly with a feminist ethics, although she does not identify herself as a feminist. Her ethic is built on the psychology of reciprocity, which promotes caring relationships as a system of exchange. Lustbader provides a spiritual as well as a psychological rationale for this system from the perspective of caregivers and those receiving care: "Mercy is based entirely on exchange. Giving help eventually embitters us, unless we are compensated at least by appreciation; accepting help degrades us, unless we are convinced that we are giving something in return. . . . Reciprocation replenishes both the spirit of the helper and the person who is helped." Such mutual compensation requires that each person knows the other and understands what life is like from his or her point of view, what theologian Martin Buber calls an "I-thou" relationship, where each party sees the other as "like me," in fact "intimately and simultaneously part of me" and yet a subject in his own right. As described by philosopher Ronald Manheimer, "I-thou" relationships create the potential for a "deeper, even higher consciousness between us than could have existed when we considered ourselves separate." Particularly in an "I-thou" relationship in which one person is vulnerable and dependent, the other has the opportunity to preserve that person's worth by helping to meet his needs, not only for the sake of the other, but "for his own sake and for what is common to both." Lustbader observes that "I-thou" relationships are very difficult for able-bodied people to develop and maintain. "Inflated" by their own health, and "distracted by the crude exterior of illness," they tend to judge others' situations on their own terms and "overlook much of the complexity going on beneath the surface."[12]

Most profoundly, Lustbader finds that a mutual exchange between partners in caregiving relationships generates hope, encouragement, and growth. Both partners gain the benefits of kindness, and the helper comes to believe that when her time of dependency comes (as it will), she, too, may be able to count on the kindness of others. She will better understand the process of decline and the lived experience of frailty and will face her own aging with less intolerance. For this reason, Lustbader entreats us all to "draw near the sickbeds": "Prior to getting sick or reaching advanced age, we can choose to grant ourselves a close acquaintance with physical suffering and its alleviation. We can draw near the sickbeds of friends and relatives and involve ourselves in the experience of helplessness, hoping that this foreknowledge will help us age well."[13]

Caring Environments in Which to Grow Old

In the late 1990s, at the time of Paul's death, 1.6 million people were living in nursing homes, 90 percent of whom were sixty-five and older, and 72 percent of whom were female. They received health-related services from 1.5 million full-time employees at an average daily rate of $213 for Medicare residents and $105 for Medicaid residents.[14] This is an expensive way to live out one's final years, and it is neither comfortable nor healthful. Today, there are 2 million people living in nursing facilities, either for short, rehabilitative periods or for longer terms, and these environments often have a "powerfully negative impact" on the residents and their families.[15] In *It Shouldn't Be This Way: The Failure of Long-Term Care*, the gerontologist Robert L. Kane, an academic expert on long-term care, and his sister Joan C. West recount their own misfortunes in placing their disabled mother in a care facility. Despite all their knowledge and experience, the authors still found the care system difficult to manage. They argue that major systemic change is needed to create more caring environments for the old and their families in America. This will require significant changes in social attitudes and public policies, including placing long-term care high on the national political agenda; putting more money into long-term care reform; providing better training, compensation, and status for care workers; and promoting stronger consumer advocacy in regards to developing more caring environments.[16]

If health care reform advocates like Kane and West are successful, within the next twenty years, older Americans will have many more choices besides the nursing home. We all stand to benefit from learning about these alternatives and supporting them: the Health Insurance Association of America estimates that by 2020, 12 million Americans will need long-term care, and that number will continue to rise as the average life expectancy increases.

The traditional nursing home, like the one where Paul resided, is built around an institutional model of medical care that emphasizes the treatment of illness. It is primarily a workplace structured around the staff's needs for cleanliness, order, and efficiency, rather than the residents' need for a "home." Thanks to advocacy groups working to change the culture of aging in America, such as the Pioneer Network, the National Citizens' Coalition for Nursing Home Reform, and Wellspring Innovative Solutions for Integrated Health Care, we now have voices, visions, and specific plans for creating healthier environments in which to grow old.

The Pioneer Network represents a successful grassroots movement on behalf of older adults. Its founding premise is that the American nursing home is a microcosm of America's culture of aging, which is based on a fear of illness, decline, and death. The nursing home, like the general culture, devalues elders *and* their caregivers. Nursing home residents and those who care for them are primarily women, and they are often poor. They need vocal advocates who can help change the system of long-term care and the culturing surrounding it. A nonprofit umbrella group based in Rochester, New York, the Pioneer Network strives to improve the quality of life in nursing homes by creating more livable, homelike environments. The group's mission is twofold: to promote long-term care practices that are more resident-centered and relationship-based and to transform policies and practices that affect the culture of aging in America. It works to create systemic change at the local level (in nursing homes) and the national level (in government agencies, research institutions, and social programs). The Pioneer Network was created by leaders in the nursing home reform movement, including the geriatrician William Thomas, who is one of the best-known advocates for old people in America.[17]

In the 1980s and 1990s, Thomas promoted the Eden Alternative to traditional nursing homes. Since then, he has become a "nursing home abolitionist," advocating instead for what he calls the Green House concept and, most recently, Eldershire, a multigenerational "intentional community" he is building on his own property. All of Thomas's elder communities are founded on a belief in person-centered or self-directed care and a strengths-based rather than deficit-based approach to caregiving. Thomas argues that diagnosis and treatment are not the same as "care" and that people who are old and disabled deserve much better care than they typically receive in nursing homes, even the good ones. Thomas's alternatives are modeled on homes, rather than hospitals, and involve significant changes in the physical and cultural environments, as well as changes in the staff's attitudes and practices.

In *Life Worth Living*, Thomas describes a new kind of nursing home, where "care" is understood as "helping others grow," regardless of age and ability. Thomas describes his efforts to turn standard nursing homes into more diverse "human habitats" that alleviate what he calls the "three neglected plagues" of nursing home life: loneliness, helplessness, and boredom. He does not consider these "personal problems" but a failure of the social system. Thomas created alternative environments in which residents were not so heavily sedated or restrained; administrators served as leaders and positive role models; employees felt empowered; and the atmosphere was enlivened with plants, animals, children, gardening, and other creative projects. Subsequently, in studying alternative nursing homes, researchers have found that staff members need to undergo an attitudinal shift in order to enact such changes. Many have become compliant with substandard practices and need to be taught how to recognize and respond to situations that inhibit quality care, as well as how to create conditions that promote a higher quality of life.[18]

Thomas's current initiative is to build Green Houses that take the place of nursing homes altogether. These are one-story houses designed to accommodate a small number of people in a homelike atmosphere, where staff and residents relate to one another as "family members." Green Houses are placed in real neighborhoods, where residents live as free of drugs and other restraints—medical, social, and physical—as possible and contribute in whatever ways they can to the functioning of the household. Thomas argues that living in such homes is not only conducive to better care, but also more cost effective in the long run than institutional care. Researchers are just beginning to study the effects of living and working in Green Houses. However, early indications are positive, according to Jude Rabig, national director of the Green House Project, who reports that staff turnover in the first Green Houses built in Tupelo, Mississippi, has been less than 10 percent per year, compared to a national average of 80 to 90 percent in traditional nursing homes.[19]

Surely, in these new environments, feminists and other enlightened scholars will be called upon to conduct research on the culture of diversity and its effects on the quality of life. Women dominate the nursing home culture, yet little research has been done on the adaptive strategies of either men or women in these facilities. Men are faced with the task of learning to live as a minority in an environment where most of the activities relate more to women's experiences than men's. We know very little about what it *feels* like to be a man in long-term care. In an attempt to gain such knowledge, gerontologists Sidney Moss and Miriam Moss interviewed twenty-one men in five long-term care facilities. Most of the men were over seventy-five and had backgrounds similar to Paul's: two-thirds had been skilled laborers or had managed or owned small businesses. In talking about their lives, the men said that work was still central to their sense of identity, and their continued ability to use skills developed over a lifetime provided a "strong sense of competence and continuity of self in spite of serious physical limitations." The authors also found that the men, half of whom were still married, limited their ties to other residents, choosing to put work and family above the development of new relationships. When they did interact with other residents, it was usually for instrumental reasons (pushing a wheelchair, answering questions), rather than social purposes. The authors give several possible explanations for the men's social reticence, including the limited number of cognitively alert men available for friendship; the mix of socioeconomic, religious, and cultural backgrounds among residents who prefer to "keep to their own kind"; inexperience or lack of comfort establishing cross-gender friendships of a platonic nature; pervasive homophobia; and an internalized ageism that causes men to think that establishing friendships with frail or demented residents implies that they, too, are old and vulnerable. The men did not form emotional ties with staff, either. Yet they continued to express a desire for independence, privacy, physical strength, and activity, including sexual activity, and they experienced a great sense of loss in regards to these aspects of life.[20]

Moss and Moss conclude that administrators, staff, and family members need to recognize the importance for old men of maintaining a sense of their masculine identities in long-term care facilities. For Paul, this might have meant being able to draw on previous work experiences, perhaps to oversee a greenhouse or garden or to help sell products created by other residents. He surely would have enjoyed having more alert men to talk to, although he was more sociable with the female residents than the men interviewed by Moss and Moss seem to have been. Undoubtedly, my presence in the nursing home helped Paul reestablish a sense of independence, along with a sense of masculinity and sexuality, for himself as well as in the eyes of other residents and family members.[21]

There are other important movements afoot that will help keep more of us out of nursing homes entirely, or at least delay our passage through their halls. The promotion nationwide of "livable" or "age-friendly" communities increases elders' opportunities for growing old and dying in their own homes and neighborhoods. Although the definitions of "livable communities" vary, they are generally understood to be places where all environmental elements work together to support the well-being of residents as they age. Livable communities offer multiple forms of affordable housing; provide supportive community systems and services (quality health care, emergency assistance, a variety of places to shop, good communications systems); and include several options for getting around, such as reliable public transportation and safe areas for walking. These are built environments that "enable" rather than "disable" older adults by extending both their personal independence and their ability to remain socially and civically active. The call for livable communities reflects a place-based, rather than cause-based, activism in response to the needs of an aging population. As social analyst Philip B. Stafford notes, "the policy question is not 'what do older people need?' but rather, 'what makes a good place to grow old?'"[22]

Answering this question requires studying the life world of elders by listening to and observing them, as well as including them in city planning. It also involves an imaginative shift in thinking, from seeing old people as "problems" to seeing them as social assets. Stafford shows how the asset-based metaphor leads to innovative planning and policies, including transportation programs that enable elders to reach volunteer sites; leadership training to assist elders in becoming neighborhood organizers; support for grandparents raising grandchildren; zoning programs that sponsor intergenerational housing; support for single mothers working as caregivers in long-term care; dementia care programs run by community members and involving people of all ages in the program; and hospice programs that teach all community members the meaning of a "good death." In the words of the geriatrician William Thomas, these imaginative communities will be like "gardens that grow people" and will benefit everyone: "People of all ages will live better lives when we . . . bring elders back to the heart of our society."[23]

Wherever we spend our final days, we will all need assistance in preparing for a "good death." For many of us, this means dying consciously among the people we love; being free from pain; leaving no unfinished business; being able to express ourselves openly and honestly; feeling unconditionally loved; and knowing that those we love will accept the course of the dying process, whatever it might bring. As the physician David Kuhl concludes in *What Dying People Want*, "Living fully and dying well involve enhancing one's sense of self, one's relationships with others, and one's understanding of the transcendent, the spiritual, the supernatural. And only in confronting the inevitability of death does one truly embrace life."[24] I consider it an honor to have shared Paul's final days and hours, and I hope that my presence contributed to the quality of his death.

The narrative psychologist Jerome Bruner believes that we live and die by stories, developing a narrative style over time that distinguishes us from all others. He uses the term "stylistic integrity" to talk about a good death in narrative terms: "You want somehow to relate your death to what you think of as your itinerary, that your death is going to be like your life in some way . . . the two are going to be of a piece."[25] As in life, Paul was thoughtful and communicative in death. He shared his feelings openly, and he acknowledged the feelings of others. I do believe he died with integrity.

We all need to keep in mind the storied nature of death as we develop new environments in which to grow old. We would do well to remember the healing potential in talking, writing, and storytelling within caring relationships at the end of life. Assisting elders with their life reviews could be a satisfying part of the work of caregivers, who, in our improved, age-enlightened world, will be paid handsomely, valued and respected for their labor, and revered for their contributions to society.

RUTH: Well, the book is finally done. What do you think of it?

PAUL: I think you did a good job. I'm proud of you, and I'm proud to be a part of it.

RUTH: But do you think it really *matters*? I mean, will it change anybody's mind about old age?

PAUL: It's hard to say. People don't change easily. Still, it's important to try.

RUTH: Any final words for our readers?

PAUL: Yes. Don't take yourselves so seriously! If you live, you're going to get old no matter what you do, so why worry about it? Just relax and enjoy the funny stories that we are.

EPILOGUE

"Karma, what's that?" Paul asked one day.

"Oh, a past that you share with someone—maybe even a past life—that you're working through now. Some might call it destiny."

"That's what we have. Surely, there's a reason for our being together. It was a long time coming. I waited my whole life for it. But I couldn't have recognized it until now."

For Paul, old age brought new kinds of awareness. This, above all, is what I learned from him: to keep your heart and mind open to change, all the way through to the end of life.

Most people who are not yet old believe that it will be terrible. We avoid the company of old people, and we condemn our own aging bodies. I once heard a folksinger on National Public Radio singing,

Don't let us get sick.
Don't let us get old.
Don't let us get stupid, all right?

This could be the national anthem of America in the twenty-first century. The lyrics suggest that to be happy, we must be healthy in mind and body, and we must be able to take care of ourselves—forever. It follows that living in a nursing home, where residents are multiply dependent, is surely a meaningless existence, devoid of interest, passion, and desire. We need gerontologists to teach us otherwise. Margaret Cruikshank, for example, shares a more nuanced understanding of decline and dependency: "Dependency comes in many forms, some of which do not entail powerlessness, and dependency must be distinguished from incompetence.... Most important, frailty can coexist with strengths. Someone who walks with great difficulty may have a strong voice, a strong will, or strong self-esteem."[1]

Learning to see value in ourselves and others as we age is a spiritual journey. Thomas R. Cole describes aging as a "moral and spiritual frontier because its unknowns, terrors and mysteries cannot be successfully crossed without humility and self-knowledge, without love and compassion, without acceptance of physical decline and mortality, and a sense of the sacred." This requires a shift in attitude toward "living with the flow of time rather than against it,"[2] a turn of mind that is beautifully captured in this excerpt from "A Hopi Elder Speaks":

> There is a river flowing now very fast.
> It is so great and swift, that there are those who will be afraid.
> They will try to hold onto the shore.
> They will feel they are being torn apart and will suffer greatly.
> Know the river has its destination.
> The elders say we must let go of the shore—
> Push off into the middle of the river,
> Keep our eyes open, and our heads above water.
> And I say, see who is there with you and celebrate.[3]

The spiritual journey of aging is social, as well as individual, and it begins for many of us at midlife, a point made repeatedly by cultural critic Margaret Gullette, who encourages us to decline the "decline narrative" that society regularly presents to us and recognize that we are "aged by culture" throughout our lives, although these forces accelerate at midlife. Gullette encourages us to take up "midlife progress narratives," in which we embrace change and appreciate the mystery and strangeness of life. Such counternarratives are based on a *trust in time* as the purveyor of benefits. These often include an increase in well-being, as a result of more confidence, self-esteem, courage, resilience, and self-mastery. In her first book on aging, *Safe at Last in the Middle Years*, Gullette writes that aging can be a psychic "cure" when the debilitating weaknesses of youth—fear, guilt, anger, arrogance, pessimism—are overcome. "It may be that some markedly felt decrease in the intensity of one's fear of death is the major precondition for being able to write midlife progress narratives," Gullette says of the American authors who write them. The "safe" in her title refers to a "state of mind, comprising skills and powers and certain [healing] attitudes toward time."[4] I think of *Endnotes* as a progress narrative in which a midlife woman (who is also a gerontologist) releases some of her youthful fears and, with the help of a good friend, comes to a better understanding of aging, decline, and death.

In one of my favorite feminist novels, this very theme unfolds in a dramatic and memorable way. In *The Diaries of Jane Somers*, Doris Lessing introduces us to a middle-aged woman, Jane, who has been avoiding the lessons of time. Jane's husband and her mother have both died, and in neither case was she emotionally present, nor did she grieve. Jane considers this a failing in herself, but she does not know what to do about it. By accident, she meets and befriends an old woman, Maudie, who is just like thousands of other old women who previously had been invisible to her. Through this friendship, and Maudie's physical and mental decline, Jane overcomes her fear of death and, in the process, becomes more fully conscious of the still unmet potential in her own life.

This, it seems, is the challenge of midlife and beyond: to learn to be fully present for death. First, it is the death of others, and then it is our own. Such presence is needed to bring us full circle to the end of a life that has been lived with awareness, intensity, and purpose. The theologian Thomas Moore reminds us that "almost every day we are asked to extend the range of our acquaintances with life. It is one of the several ways to live intensely, and it is also a way to prepare for death."[5] At fifty-three, thanks to my relationship with Paul, I am inclined to agree with Moore that death is merely an end to what has become familiar and an opening to something new.

ACKNOWLEDGMENTS

I thank the following for their support and encouragement over the past ten years as I wrote, rewrote, and procrastinated in writing this book.

The Brookdale Foundation for the three-year fellowship in gerontology (1994–97) during which time I came to understand and appreciate the lives of old people.

The Wayne State University Institute of Gerontology, under the directorship of Jeff Dwyer, for a nurturing intellectual environment during the course of my fellowship.

The Wayne State University College of Liberal Arts and Sciences for a sabbatical year that advanced this project considerably.

Elizabeth Chapleski, who listened without judgment, and May Berkley, who encouraged me to "just write the story."

Thomas R. Cole, friend and mentor, who has always shown respect for my feelings, as well as my thoughts.

Gwen Gorzelsky, friend and colleague, who commented on early notes and expressed enduring faith in the value of this project.

Virginia Richardson, who took a chance on promoting this unorthodox book for the End-of-Life Series at Columbia University Press.

Roy D. Atkinson, friend and business-partner-in-debt, for his humor and patience during these many years of writing.

NOTES

Preface

1. Nancy K. Miller, *Bequest and Betrayal: Memoirs of a Parent's Death* (Bloomington: Indiana University Press, 1996), x–xi.

2. Ibid., 2.

3. Wayne Campbell Peck, Linda Flower, and Lorraine Higgins, "Community Literacy," *College Composition and Communication* 46, no. 2 (1995): 199–222.

4. Harry R. Moody, "Overview: What Is Critical Gerontology and Why Is It Important?" in Thomas R. Cole, W. Andrew Achenbaum, Patricia L. Jakobi, and Robert Kastenbaum, eds. *Voices and Visions of Aging: Toward a Critical Gerontology* (New York: Springer, 1993), xv–xli; emphasis in original.

5. For an articulation of feminist gerontology, see Toni Calasanti and Kathleen Slevin, *Age Matters: Realigning Feminist Thinking* (New York: Routledge, 2006).

6. Malcolm Cowley, *The View from 80* (New York: Viking, 1980), ix.

7. Ruth E. Ray, "Narratives as Agents of Social Change: A New Direction for Narrative Gerontologists," in Miriam Bernard and Thomas Scharf, eds., *Critical Perspectives on Ageing Societies* (Bristol, UK: Policy Press, 2007), 60.

1. Passionate Scholarship

1. Martha B. Holstein and Meredith Minkler, "Critical Gerontology: Reflections for the 21st Century," in Miriam Bernard and Thomas Scharf, eds., *Critical Perspectives on Ageing Societies* (Bristol, UK: Policy Press, 2007), 26.

2. Ruth E. Ray, "Narratives as Agents of Social Change: A New Direction for Narrative Gerontologists," in Bernard and Scharf, 59–72; emphasis in original.

3. Valerie Barnes Lipscomb, "'We Need a Theoretical Base': Cynthia Rich, Women's Studies, and Ageism" (an interview with Cynthia Rich), *NWSA Journal* 18, no. 1: 3.

4. Carroll L. Estes, Elizabeth A. Binney, and Richard A. Culbertson, "The Gerontological Imagination: Social Influences on the Development of Gerontology, 1945–Present," *International Journal of Aging and Human Development* 35, no. 1 (1992): 58–59.

5. Ibid., 60–63.

6. C. Wright Mills, *The Sociological Imagination*, 40th anniv. ed. (New York: Oxford University Press, 2000), 195–97.

7. Ibid., 219.

8. Laurel Richardson, *Fields of Play: Constructing an Academic Life* (New Brunswick, N.J.: Rutgers University, 1997), 58, 49, 168.

9. Toril Moi, *What Is a Woman?* (New York: Oxford University, 1999), 120, 165.

10. Ibid., 123, 129.

11. Gesa Kirsch, *Ethical Dilemmas in Feminist Research: The Politics of Location, Interpretation, and Publication* (Albany: SUNY Press, 1999), 3–4.

12. Tom L. Beauchamp and James F. Childress, *Principles of Biomedical Ethics*, 5th ed. (New York: Oxford University Press, 2001), summarized in G. Thomas Couser, *Vulnerable Subjects: Ethics and Life Writing* (Ithaca: Cornell University Press, 2004), 27.

13. Couser, ix.

14. Ibid., x–xi.

15. Ibid., x.

16. Kamala Visweswaran, *Fictions of Feminist Ethnography* (Minneapolis: University of Minnesota Press, 1994), 32.

2. Home

1. For further information on nursing homes, see *Vital and Health Statistics*, ser. 13, no. 152, "The National Nursing Home Survey: 1999 Summary" (Hyattsville, Md.: U.S. Department of Health and Human Services, National Center for Health Statistics, June 2002). For more current information from the perspective of nursing home directors, see the Online Nursing Homes Direction Web site at www.omniknowledge.org, "Nursing Homes."

2. See Katherine P. Supiano, Ronald J. Ozminkowski, Ruth Campbell, and Carole Lapidos, "Effectiveness of Writing Groups in Nursing Homes," *Journal of Applied Gerontology* 8 (1989): 382–400. Pre- and post-tests of affect, depression, and cognitive functioning were given to participants in several writing groups that met for eight weeks, as well as a control group. The authors found that participation in a writing group promoted positive changes in nursing home residents and that those who benefited most were the severely depressed and cognitively impaired.

For less scientific descriptions of writers, writing, and writing groups in nursing homes, see Marc Kaminsky, *What's Inside You It Shines Out of You* (New York: Horizon Press, 1974), and Kaminsky, ed. *The Uses of Reminiscence: New Ways of Working with Older Adults* (New York: Haworth, 1984); Kenneth Koch, *I Never Told Anybody: Teaching Poetry Writing in a Nursing Home* (New York: Random House, 1977); and Lenore Coberly, Jeri McCormick, and Karen Updike, *Writers Have No Age: Creative Writing with Older Adults* (New York: Haworth Press, 1984). Nonprofit organizations such as the Foxfire Fund in Rabun County, Ga.; the Legacy Center in Minneapolis; the Jewish Community Foundation in San Diego; and San Francisco's Eldergivers have sponsored and published oral history and autobiographical projects with residents of nursing homes.

3. Making Ourselves Understood

1. Nursing home theft is a form of elder abuse about which very little has been written in the gerontological literature. In a survey of 281 anonymous

employees at six nursing homes in the southeastern United States, researchers at the University of Tennessee found that 3.9 percent reported they had taken something from a resident, and 37.3 percent reported that they had observed someone else take something from a resident. (The researchers acknowledge that because of the sensitive nature of the questionnaire, the data likely reflect some degree of underreporting.) Of those who reported observing thefts by others, 9.7 percent said they saw a staff member steal and 33.5 percent said they saw a resident steal from another resident. A few reported seeing both staff and residents steal. The item stolen most often was money.

The researchers concluded that attitudes toward work, residents, and theft are interrelated. Staff (including maintenance, housekeeping, and food service workers, as well as nursing aides) are more likely to steal when they are dissatisfied with their jobs, hold negative attitudes toward residents, and/or hold positive attitudes toward stealing from residents. See Diana K. Harris and Michael Benson, "Nursing Home Theft: The Hidden Problem," *Journal of Aging Studies* 12, no. 1 (1998): 57–67.

2. The feminist critic bell hooks, in *Communion: The Female Search for Love* (New York: W. Morrow, 2002), suggests that professional women of my generation who were strongly focused on building careers during the first half of their lives often chose emotionally unavailable men so that they wouldn't feel engulfed by relationships and distracted from their goals. Around the age of forty, however, many career women begin to seek relationships that require more emotional involvement. Other feminist writers who reflect on midlife career women's search for deeper emotional and spiritual connections include Jean Shinoda Bolen, *Crossing to Avalon: A Woman's Midlife Pilgrimage* (San Francisco: HarperSanFrancisco, 1994), and Sue Monk Kidd, *The Dance of the Dissident Daughter: A Woman's Journey from Christian Tradition to the Sacred Feminine* (San Francisco: HarperSanFrancisco, 1996).

4. New Year's Eve

1. Data from the National Kidney and Urologic Diseases Information Clearinghouse (www.kidney.niddk.nih.gov), accessed April 20, 2007, indicate that 20 to 46 percent of men age forty to sixty-nine self-reported moderate or com-

plete erectile dysfunction (impotence). Impotence, either moderate or complete, in men age seventy and over is likely much higher. Prostate cancer is a common cause. In 2002, there were approximately 1.8 million American men living with prostate cancer.

Enlightened critics provide new ways to respond to these statistics. Some feminists have argued that impotence in America is largely a medical construction based on the phallocentric concept of male sexuality as centered exclusively around the penis. Feminists invite us to think beyond this construction to envision broader, more encompassing expressions of male sexuality. For a critique of medical and social constructions of impotence, see Lenore Tiefer, "The Medicalization of Impotence: Normalizing Phallocentrism," *Gender and Society* 8, no. 3 (1994): 363–77.

For a thoughtful discussion of alternative forms of sexual expression in later life, see Robert N. Butler and Myrna I. Lewis, *The New Love and Sex after 60* (New York: Ballantine, 2002).

5. A Lamentable Situation

1. See www.lifespan.org, an informational Web site sponsored by Lifespan, a partnership of five hospitals in Rhode Island, for diagnosis, symptoms, research findings, and the most up-to-date treatments for Parkinson's disease.

2. J. Thomas Hutton and Raye Lynne Dippel, eds., *Caring for the Parkinson Patient: A Practical Guide* (Buffalo: Prometheus Books, 1989). For a more personal account of the experience of Parkinson's, see Joel Havemann, *A Life Shaken: My Encounter with Parkinson's Disease* (Baltimore: Johns Hopkins University Press, 2002).

7. Passion's Progress

1. A written care plan is mandated in the regulations and routines of American nursing homes. Typically, the resident assessment instrument/minimum data set provides the basis for developing a care plan for each resident. This plan is periodically revisited through scheduled care conferences that may involve the

resident, family members, the nursing home administrator, the director of nursing, the staff social worker, and one or more certified nursing assistants. For the history and rationale of care plans, see Mary Ellen Dellefield, "Interdisciplinary Care Planning and the Written Care Plan in Nursing Homes: A Critical Review," *Gerontologist* 46 (2006): 128–33.

8. Activities

1. Stephen Katz, "Busy Bodies: Activity, Aging, and the Management of Everyday Life," *Journal of Aging Studies* 14 (2000): 135–52.

2. Margaret Cruikshank, *Learning to be Old: Gender, Culture, and Aging* (Lanham, Md.: Rowman and Littlefield, 2003), 171.

3. William H. Thomas, *Life Worth Living: How Someone You Love Can Still Enjoy Life in a Nursing Home: The Eden Alternative in Action* (Acton, Mass.: VanderWyk and Burnham, 1996); Lars Tornstam, *Gerotranscendence: A Developmental Theory of Positive Aging* (New York: Springer, 2005).

4. Nancy Foner, *The Caregiving Dilemma: Work in an American Nursing Home* (Berkeley: University of California, 1994), 54–59.

9. Diaper Is a Dirty Word

1. The U.S. National Kidney and Urologic Diseases Information Clearinghouse reports that in 2000, nearly 25 percent of Caucasian men between the ages of fifty and seventy-nine—6.5 million men—were expected to be diagnosed with benign prostatic hyperplasia (BPH) or enlarged prostate, which affects bladder functioning. Some treatments for prostate cancer can cause incontinence. Common remedies include behavior modification (exercising the pelvic muscles, biofeedback, timed voiding, bladder training), medications, and, if none of these work, urethral injections or artificial sphincters, which keep the urethra closed until the time of elimination, or catheters, which are drainage systems. The "water pill" that Paul spoke of may have been a diuretic used to treat high blood pressure. Such pills reduce fluid in the body by increasing urine produc-

tion. For information on diagnosis and treatment of urinary incontinence, see www.kidney.niddk.nih.gov.

11. Empty Rooms

1. Wayne Booth, ed., *The Art of Growing Older: Writers on Living and Aging* (Chicago: University of Chicago, 1992), 88.

12. Ethics of Care

1. Arthur P. Bochner and Janet Rushing, "Breathing Life into Work," in Carolyn Ellis and Arthur P. Bochner, eds., *Composing Ethnography: Alternative Forms of Qualitative Writing* (Walnut Creek, Calif.: AltaMira Press, 1996), 218; Wayne Booth, "The Ethics of Medicine, as Revealed in Literature," in Rita Charon and Martha Montello, eds., *Stories Matter: The Role of Narrative in Medical Ethics* (New York: Routledge, 2002), 11; Robert Coles, *The Call of Stories: Teaching and the Moral Imagination* (Boston: Houghton Mifflin, 1989); Thomas R. Cole, "Introduction: The Multiple Meanings of Stories: Scholarship, Self-Knowledge, Cultural Transmission, Public Service, and the Sacred," in Marc Kaminsky, Mark Weiss, and Deena Metzger, eds., *Stories as Equipment for Living: Last Talks and Tales of Barbara Myerhoff* (Ann Arbor: University of Michigan Press, 2007).

2. bell hooks, *Communion: The Female Search for Love* (New York: W. Morrow, 2002,) xviii.

3. Thomas Moore, *Original Self: Living with Paradox and Originality* (New York: HarperCollins, 2000), 74.

4. hooks, 77, 175; emphasis added.

5. Virginia Held, *The Ethics of Care: Personal, Political, and Global* (New York: Oxford University Press, 2006), 14.

6. Ibid., 42, 55.

7. Margaret Urban Walker, "Moral Understandings: Alternative 'Epistemology' for a Feminist Ethics" (1989), rpt. in Virginia Held, ed., *Justice and Care:*

Essential Readings in Feminist Ethics (Boulder, Colo.: Westview, 1995), 142; Robin Fiore, preface in Held, *Justice and Care*, ix.

8. Daryl Koehn, *Rethinking Feminist Ethics: Care, Trust, and Empathy* (London: Routledge, 1998), 8.

9. Held, *Ethics of Care*, 56.

10. Margaret Urban Walker, qtd. in Held, *Ethics of Care*, 50.

11. Wendy Lustbader, *Counting on Kindness: The Dilemmas of Dependency* (New York: Free Press, 1991), xiii, 15; Thomas R. Cole, "Is Bioethics Tethering the Gerontological Imagination?" paper delivered at 59th Annual Meeting of the Gerontological Society of America, November 17, 2006, Dallas, Tex.

12. Lustbader, 18, 38; Ronald Manheimer, *A Map to the End of Time: Wayfarings with Friends and Philosophers* (New York: Norton, 1999), 50.

13. Lustbader, 170.

14. Adrienne Jones, *National Nursing Home Survey: 1999 Summary* (Hyattsville, Md.: U.S. Department of Health and Human Services, Centers for Disease Control and Prevention, National Center for Health Statistics, 2002).

15. Lois J. Cutler, Rosalie A. Kane, Howard B. Degenholtz, Michael J. Miller, and Leslie Grant, "Assessing and Comparing Physical Environments for Nursing Home Residents: Using New Tools for Greater Research Specificity," *Gerontologist* 46 (2006): 42–51.

16. Robert L. Kane and Joan C. West, *It Shouldn't Be This Way: The Failure of Long-Term Care* (Nashville: Vanderbilt University, 2005).

17. For more information on the Pioneer Network, see Audrey S. Weiner and Judah L. Ronch, *Culture Change in Long-Term Care* (New York: Haworth Press, 2003). See also the Pioneer Network Web site www.pioneernetwork.net.

For information on the Wellspring Change Model, which focuses on resident-directed care and staff empowerment to improve quality of life in nursing homes, see Wellspring Innovative Solutions for Integrated Health Care at www.wellspringis.org. According to the Web site ("Our Story"), Wellspring homes have decreased the number of bed-bound residents and rely less on restraints and psychoactive drugs. Their residents also resist infections better and experience less incontinence.

18. William H. Thomas, *Life Worth Living: How Someone You Love Can Still Enjoy Life in a Nursing Home: The Eden Alternative in Action* (Acton, Mass.: VanderWyk and Burnham, 1996), . For information on overcoming attitudinal barriers to change, see Lois J. Cutler and Rosalie A. Kane's workbook

Practical Strategies to Transform Nursing Home Environments: Towards Better Quality of Life (Minneapolis: University of Minnesota, National Long-Term Care Research Center, 2004).

19. Qtd. in William L. Hamilton, "The New Nursing Home, Emphasis on Home," *New York Times*, April 23, 2005.

20. Sidney Z. Moss and Miriam S. Moss, "Being a Man in Long-Term Care," *Journal of Aging Studies* 21 (2007): 43–54; "strong sense . . ." is on 47.

21. Ibid., 52.

22. Andrew Kochera and Kim Bright, "Livable Communities for Older People," *Generations* (Winter 2005–6): 32–36; Philip B. Stafford, "Creating Lifespan Communities," *Public Policy and Aging Report* 15, no. 4: 8.

23. For more information on livable communities, see *Beyond 50.05: A Report to the Nation on Livable Communities: Creating Environments for Successful Aging* (Washington, D.C.: AARP, 2005). Thomas qtd. in Caroline Hsu, "The Greening of Aging," *U.S. News & World Report*, June 19, 2006, 48–52.

24. David Kuhl, *What Dying People Want: Practical Wisdom for the End of Life* (N.p.: Anchor Canada, 2003), 290–91.

25. Jerome Bruner, "Narratives of Human Plight: A Conversation with Jerome Bruner," in Charon and Montello, 5.

Epilogue

1. Margaret Cruikshank, *Learning to Be Old: Gender, Culture, and Aging* (Lanham, Md.: Rowman and Littlefield, 2003), 14–15.

2. Thomas R. Cole, *The Journey of Life: A Cultural History of Aging in America* (Cambridge: Cambridge University Press, 1992), 243; Cole, "On the Possibilities of Spirituality and Religious Humanism in Gerontology" in Melvin Kimble and Susan McFadden, eds. *Aging, Spirituality, and Religion* (Minneapolis: Fortress Press, 2003), 2:434–48.

3. "A Hopi Elder Speaks," courtesy of Second Journey, the North Carolina–based organization working on behalf of conscious aging. Visit their Web site at www.SecondJourney.net.

4. See Margaret Morganroth Gullette, *Declining to Decline: Cultural Combat and the Politics of the Midlife* (Charlottesville: University Press of Virginia, 1997); Gullette, *Aged by Culture* (Chicago: University of Chicago Press, 2004);

and Gullette, *Safe at Last in the Middle Years: The Invention of the Midlife Progress Novel* (Berkeley: University of California Press, 1988), quotes are from pp. 39 and 24, respectively.

5. Thomas Moore, *Original Self: Living with Paradox and Originality* (New York: HarperCollins, 2000), 25.